AN ALEXANDRIA
ANTHOLOGY

AN ALEXANDRIA ANTHOLOGY

Travel Writing through the Centuries

Edited by
Michael Haag

The American University in Cairo Press
Cairo New York

To Hunter Rogers, cousin and friend

Copyright © 2014 by
The American University in Cairo Press
113 Sharia Kasr el Aini, Cairo, Egypt
420 Fifth Avenue, New York, NY 10018
www.aucpress.com

Exclusive distribution outside Egypt and North America by I.B. Tauris & Co Ltd.,
6 Salem Road, London, W2 4BU

Dar el Kutub No. 2316/14
ISBN 978 977 416 672 3

Dar el Kutub Cataloging-in-Publication Data

Haag, Michael
        An Alexandria Anthology: Travel Writing through the Centuries /
Michael Haag.—Cairo: The American University in Cairo Press, 2014.
        p.   cm.
        ISBN 978 977 416 672 3
        1.   Egypt—Description and travel
        2.   Alexandria (Egypt—Description and travel)
        I.   Title
        916.2116

1 2 3 4 5   18 17 16 15 14

Designed by Fatiha Bouzidi
Printed in Egypt

Contents

The Ancient City

For nearly a thousand years after its founding by Alexander the Great in 331 BC Alexandria was one of the great cultural and intellectual centers of the world, a city universal and cosmopolitan. Alexandria's Museum, of which the Library was a part, and the towering Pharos lighthouse, have remained symbols of enlightenment to this day.

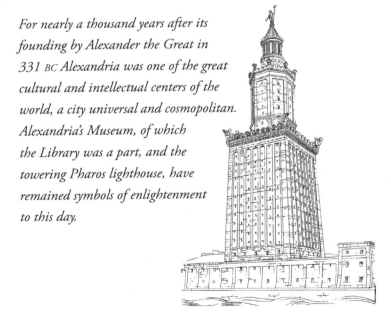

Alexander the Great Founds Alexandria, 331 BC
Plutarch

The Persians overran the Middle East, including Egypt, and twice attempted to invade Greece but were repulsed. Alexander the Great launched a counterattack, and in 331 BC, after driving the Persians out of Egypt, he founded a new city on the Mediterranean shore.

After his conquest of Egypt, Alexander wished to found a large and populous Greek city which should bear his name, and by the advice of his architects was on the point of measuring off and enclosing a certain site for it. Then, in the night, as he lay asleep, he saw a wonderful vision. A man with very hoary locks and of a venerable aspect appeared to stand by his side and recite these lines from Homer's *Odyssey* —

There is an island in the surging sea, which they call Pharos, lying off Egypt. It has a harbour with good anchorage, and hence they put out to sea after drawing water.

Accordingly, he rose up at once and went to Pharos, which at that time was still an island, a little above the Canopic mouth of the Nile, but now it has been joined to the mainland by a causeway. And when he saw a site of surpassing natural advantages (for it is a strip of land like enough to a broad isthmus, extending between a great lagoon and a stretch of sea which terminates in a large harbour), he said he saw now that Homer was not only admirable in other ways, but also a very wise architect, and ordered the plan of the city to be drawn in conformity with this site.

There was no chalk at hand, so they took barley-meal and marked out with it on the dark soil a rounded area, to whose inner arc straight lines extended so as to produce the figure of a *chlamys*, or military cloak, the lines beginning from the skirts (as one may say), and narrowing the breadth of the area uniformly. The king was delighted with the design; but suddenly birds from the river and the lagoon, infinite in number and of every sort and size, settled down upon the place like clouds and devoured every particle of the barley-meal, so that even Alexander was greatly disturbed at the omen. However, the seers exhorted him to be of good cheer, since the city here founded by him would have most abundant and helpful resources and be a nursing mother for men of every nation, and so he ordered those in charge of the work to proceed with it.

Alexandria Described, early 1st century AD
Strabo

The Great Harbor described by Strabo is the Eastern Harbor of today; Fort Qaytbay stands on the site of the Pharos lighthouse on its western arm, and Cape Lochias is the promontory to the east, jutting out in front of the modern Bibliotheca Alexandrina. The royal palaces, the Museum, and the Library filled all the sweep of the harbor from Cape Lochias to approximately the site of the present-day Hotel Cecil, which stands close to the site of the Caesareum, in front of which once stood Cleopatra's Needles. The Heptastadium was a causeway built to connect the island of Pharos to the mainland and which has since silted up and is built upon; beyond it lies the Harbor of Eunostos (Safe Return),

today's Western Harbor, which is modern Alexandria's com-
mercial port. The broad street described by Strabo as running
from Necropolis in the east to the Canopic Gate and beyond
it to Nicopolis in the west is followed by Sharia al-Hurriya,
Alexandria's main street today. But apart from the outline
of the harbors and the traces of the streets, almost nothing
remains of ancient Alexandria. Strabo makes no mention of
Pompey's Pillar, which had not yet been erected.

The advantages of the city's site are various; for, first, the
place is washed by two seas, on the north by the Egyptian
Sea, as it is called, and on the south by Lake Mareotis.
This is filled by many canals from the Nile, both from
above and on the sides, and through these canals the
imports are much larger than those from the sea, so that
the harbour on the lake was in fact richer than that on
the sea; and here the exports from Alexandria also are
larger than the imports. . . .

In addition to the great value of the things brought
down from both directions, both into the harbour on the
sea and into that on the lake, the salubrity of the air is

also worthy of remark. And this likewise results from the fact that the land is washed by water on both sides and because of the timeliness of the Nile's risings; for the other cities that are situated on lakes have heavy and stifling air in the heats of summer, because the lakes then become marshy along their edges because of the evaporation caused by the sun's rays, and, accordingly, when so much filth-laden moisture rises, the air inhaled is noisome and starts pestilential diseases, whereas at Alexandria, at the beginning of summer, the Nile, being full, fills the lake also, and leaves no marshy matter to corrupt the rising vapours. At that time, also, the Etesian winds blow from the north and from a vast sea, so that the Alexandrians pass their time most pleasantly in summer. . . .

The city as a whole is intersected by streets practicable for horse-riding and chariot-driving, and by two that are very broad, extending to more than a plethrum in breadth, which cut one another into two sections and at right angles. And the city contains most beautiful public precincts and also the royal palaces, which constitute one-fourth or even one-third of the whole circuit of the city; for just as each of the kings, from love of splendour, was wont to add some adornment to the public monuments, so also he would invest himself at his own expense with a residence, in addition to those already built, so that now, to quote the words of the poet, "there is building upon building." All, however, are connected with one another and the harbour, even those that lie outside the harbour.

The Museum is also a part of the royal palaces; it has a public walk, an Exedra with seats, and a large house, in which is the common mess-hall of the men of learning who share the Museum. This group of men not only hold property in common, but also have a priest in charge of the Museum, who formerly was appointed by the kings, but is now appointed by Caesar. The Sema also, as it is called, is a part of the royal palaces. This was the enclosure which contained the burial-places of the kings and that of Alexander. . . .

In the Great Harbour at the entrance, on the right hand, are the island and the tower Pharos, and on the other hand are the reefs and also the promontory Lochias, with a royal palace upon it; and on sailing into the harbour one comes, on the left, to the inner royal palaces, which are continuous with those on Lochias and have groves and numerous lodges painted in various colours.

Below these lies the harbour that was dug by the hand of man and is hidden from view, the private property of the kings, as also Antirrhodos, an isle lying off the artificial harbour, which has both a royal palace and a small harbour. They so called it as being a rival of Rhodes. Above the artificial harbour lies the theatre; then the Poseidium—an elbow, as it were, projecting from the Emporium, as it is called, and containing a temple of Poseidon. To this elbow of land Antony added a mole projecting still farther, into the middle of a harbour, and on the extremity of it built a royal lodge which he called Timonium. This was his last act, when, forsaken by his friends, he sailed away to Alexandria after his misfortune at Actium, having chosen to live the life of a Timon to the end of his days, which he intended to spend in solitude from all those friends. Then one comes to the Caesareum and the Emporium and the warehouses; and after these to the ship-houses, which extend as far as the Heptastadium. So much for the Great Harbour and its surroundings.

Next, after the Heptastadium, one comes to the Harbour of Eunostus, and, above this, to the artificial harbour, which is also called Cibotus; it too has ship-houses. Farther in there is a navigable canal, which extends to Lake Mareotis. Now outside the canal there is still left only a small part of the city; and then one comes to the suburb Necropolis, in which are many gardens and groves and halting-places fitted up for the embalming of corpses, and, inside the canal, both to the Serapeum and to other sacred precincts of ancient times, which are now almost abandoned on account of the construction of the new buildings at Nicopolis; for instance, there are an amphitheatre and a stadium at Nicopolis, and the quinquennial games are celebrated there; but the ancient buildings have fallen into neglect.

In short, the city is full of public and sacred structures; but the most beautiful is the Gymnasium, which has porticoes more than a stadium in length. And in the middle are both the court of justice and the groves. Here, too, is the Paneium, a "height," as it were, which was made by the hand of man; it has the shape of a fir-cone, resembles a rocky hill, and is ascended by a spiral road; and from the summit one can see the whole of the city lying below it on all sides.

The broad street that runs lengthwise extends from Necropolis past the Gymnasium to the Canopic Gate; and then one comes to the Hippodrome, as it is called, and to the other streets that lie parallel, extending as far as the Canopic canal. Having passed through the Hippodrome, one comes to Nicopolis, which has a settlement on the sea no smaller than a city. It is thirty stadia distant from Alexandria. Augustus Caesar honoured this place because it was here that he conquered in battle those who came out against him with Antony; and when he had taken the city at the first onset, he forced Antony to put himself to death and Cleopatra to come into his power alive; but a little later she too put herself to death secretly, while in prison, by the bite of an asp or (for two accounts are given) by applying a poisonous ointment;

and the result was that the empire of the sons of Lagus, which had endured for many years, was dissolved.

Spectacle at the Crossroads of the World, early 2nd century AD
Dio of Prusa

My friends, would you kindly be serious for a brief while and give heed to my words? For you are forever being frivolous and heedless, and you are practically never at a loss for fun-making and enjoyment and laughter—indeed you have many who minister to such tendencies—but I find in you a complete lack of seriousness. . . .

Your city is vastly superior in point of size and situation, and it is admittedly ranked second among all cities beneath the sun. For not only does the mighty nation, Egypt, constitute the framework of your city—or more accurately its appendage—but the peculiar nature of the river, when compared with all others, defies description with regard to both its marvellous habits and its usefulness; and furthermore, not only have you a monopoly of the shipping of the entire Mediterranean by reason of the beauty of your harbours, the magnitude of your fleet, and the abundance and the marketing of the products of every land, but also the outer waters that lie beyond are in your grasp, both the Red Sea and the Indian Ocean, whose name was rarely heard in former days. The result is that the trade, not merely of islands, ports, a few straits and isthmuses, but of practically the whole world is yours. For Alexandria is situated, as it were, at the cross-roads of the whole world, of even the most remote nations thereof, as if it were a market serving a single city, a market which brings together into one place all manner of men, displaying them to one another and, as far as possible, making them a kindred people. . . .

What I said just now about the city was meant to show you that whatever impropriety you commit is committed, not in secrecy or in the presence of just a few, but in the presence of all mankind. For I behold among you, not merely Greeks and Italians and people from neighbouring Syria, Libya, Cilicia, nor yet Ethiopians and Arabs from more distant regions, but even Bactrians and Scythians and Persians and a few Indians, and all these help to make up the audience in your theatre and sit beside you on each occasion; therefore, while you, perchance, are listening to a single harpist, and that too a man with whom you are well acquainted, you are being listened to by countless peoples who do not know you; and while you are watching three or four charioteers, you yourselves are being watched by countless Greeks and barbarians as well.

What, then, do you suppose those people say when they have returned to their homes at the ends of the earth? Do they not say: "We have seen a city that in most respects is admirable and a spectacle that surpasses all human spectacles, with regard both to beauty and sanctuaries and multitude of inhabitants and abundance of all that man requires," going on to describe to their fellow citizens as accurately as possible all the things that I myself named a short while ago—all about the Nile, the land, and the sea, and in particular the epiphany of the god; "and yet," they will add, "it is a city that is mad over music and horse-races and in these matters behaves in a manner entirely unworthy of itself. For the Alexandrians are moderate enough when they offer sacrifice or stroll by themselves or engage in their other pursuits; but when they enter the theatre or the stadium, just as if drugs that would madden them lay buried there, they lose all consciousness of their former state and are not ashamed to say or do anything that occurs to them. And what is most distressing of all is that, despite their interest in the show, they do not really see, and, though they wish to hear, they do not hear, being evidently out of their senses and deranged—not only men, but even women and children. And when the dreadful exhibition is over and they are dismissed, although the more violent aspect of their disorder has been extinguished, still at street-corners and in alley-ways the malady continues throughout the entire city for several days; just as when a mighty conflagration has died down, you can see for a long time, not only the smoke, but also some portions of the buildings still aflame."

Wine and Song on Lake Mareotis, 1st century AD
Anthony de Cosson

It was the custom of the people of Alexandria to spend their holidays on the lake, sailing in boats provided with cabins, and they would sail in under the shade of the great bean leaves and make merry. Near Abu Sir, close to the sea, was a rocky spot which was the resort of great numbers of people at all seasons of the year for the purpose of recreation on holidays, so Strabo tells us. Good Mareotic wine and beer could be obtained at the towns on the lake—at Nicium, Mareotis, Plinthine, Taposiris, and at the little inns on the islands where, perhaps, there were benches under the vine trellises. There the gay boating parties would put in for refreshment. On such feast-days one can picture the western arm of Mareotis, between the low hills, lit up with white sails by day and the reflections of lamps by night; while, as the boats returned towards Alexandria in the evening, one heard, carried across the dark waters, the sound of voices singing.

Medieval Impressions

The Arabs invaded Egypt in 640 and
captured Alexandria in 642. The city amazed
them, but under their rule it declined. Instead
they built a new capital at Fustat, part of
present-day Cairo.

From the Arab Conqueror of Egypt
to the Caliph Umar in Arabia, 642
Amr ibn al-As

I have taken a city of which I can but say that it contains 4000 palaces, 4000 baths, 400 theatres, 12,000 sellers of green vegetables and 40,000 tributary Jews.

Terrestrial Delight, c.760
Abd al-Malik ibn Juraij

I have made the pilgrimage sixty times; but if God had suffered me to stay a month at Alexandria and pray on its shores, that month would be dearer to me than the sixty prescribed pilgrimages which I have undertaken.

For the Glory of God, 1183
Ibn Jubayr

First there is the fine situation of the city, and the spaciousness of its buildings. We have never seen a town with broader streets, or higher structures, or one more ancient and beautiful. Its markets also are magnificent. A remarkable thing about the construction of the city is that the buildings below the ground are like those above it and are even finer and stronger, because the waters of the Nile wind underground beneath the houses and alleyways. The wells are connected, and flow into each other. We observed many marble columns and slabs of height, amplitude, and splendour such as cannot be imagined. You will find in some of its avenues columns that climb up to and choke the skies, and whose purpose and the reason for whose erection none can tell. It was related to us that in ancient times they supported a building reserved for philosophers and the chief men of the day. God knows best, but they seem to be for the purpose of astronomical observations.

One of the greatest wonders that we saw in this city was the lighthouse which Great and Glorious God had erected by the hands of those who were forced to such labour as "a sign to those who take warning from examining the fate of others" [Qur'an 15:75] and as a guide to voyagers, for without it they could not find the true course to Alexandria. It can be seen for more than seventy miles, and is of great antiquity. It is most strongly built in all directions and competes with the skies in height. Description of it falls short, the eyes fail to comprehend it, and words are inadequate, so vast is the spectacle.

We measured one of its four sides and found it to be more than fifty arms' lengths. It is said that in height it is more than one hundred and fifty *qamah* [1 *qamah* = the height of a man]. Its interior is an awe-inspiring sight in its amplitude, with stairways and entrances and numerous apartments, so that he who penetrates and wanders through its passages may be lost. In short, words fail to give a conception of it. May God not let it cease to be an affirmation of Islam and for that creed preserve it. At its summit is a mosque having the qualities of blessedness, for men are blessed by praying therein. . . . We went up to this blessed mosque and prayed in it. We saw such marvels of construction as cannot faithfully be described.

The Final Destruction of the Serapeum, c.1200
Abd al-Latif al-Baghdadi

I saw at Alexandria the column named Amoud-alsawari ['the Column of the Horseman,' but also known at the time as the Column of the Pillars, later known as Pompey's Pillar]. It is of granite, of red stone, which is extremely hard. This column is a surpassing size and height: I had no difficulty in believing it was seventy cubits high; its diameter is five cubits; it is raised on a very large base proportional to its size. On top of this column is a big capital, which could not be so well positioned with such accuracy without a deep knowledge of mechanics and the art of raising great weights, and extreme skill in practical geometry. A man worthy of trust assured me that he measured the periphery of this column and found it was seventy-five spans of your large measure.

I also saw on the seashore, on the side where it borders the walls of the city, over four hundred columns broken into two or three parts, of which the stone was similar to that used by the Column of the Pillars [Pompey's Pillar] and which seemed to be to it in the proportion of a third or a fourth. All the residents of Alexandria, without exception, assume that the columns were erected around the Column of the Pillars; but a governor of Alexandria named Karadja, who commanded in this city for Yusuf son of Ayyub [Saladin], saw fit to overthrow these columns, to break them and throw them on the edge of the sea, under the pretext of breaking the force of the waves and thereby protecting the city walls from their violence, or to prevent enemy ships from anchoring against the walls. This was acting like a child, or man who cannot distinguish right from wrong.

Ruins and Wonders, 1326–49
Ibn Battuta

At length on April 5th [1326] we reached Alexandria. It is a beautiful city, well-built and fortified with four gates and a magnificent port. . . .

I went to see the lighthouse on this occasion and found one of its faces in ruins. It is a very high square building, and its door is above the level of the earth. Opposite the door, and of the same height, is a building from which there is a plank bridge to the door; if this is removed there is no means of entrance. Inside the door is a place for the lighthouse-keeper, and within the lighthouse there are many chambers. The breadth of the passage inside is nine spans and that of the wall ten spans; each of the four sides of the lighthouse is 140 spans in breadth. It is situated on a high mound and lies three miles from the city on a long tongue of land which juts out into the sea from close by the city wall, so that the lighthouse cannot be reached by land except from the city. On my return to the West in the year 750 [1349] I visited the lighthouse again, and found that it had fallen into so ruinous a condition that it was not possible to enter it or climb up to the door. . . .

Another of the marvellous things in this city is the awe-inspiring marble column on its outskirts which they call the Column of the Pillars [Pompey's Pillar]. It is a single block, skilfully carved, erected on a plinth of square stones like enormous platforms, and no one knows how it was erected there nor for certain who erected it.

Early European Travelers

Adventurous European travelers began visiting Alexandria in the sixteenth century, only to discover that very little survived of the city's resplendent past. Decline under the Arabs was followed by the Turkish invasion of Egypt in 1517, which turned the country into a neglected provincial backwater of the Ottoman Empire. Also, ever since Portugal's Vasco da Gama found the way to India around Africa in 1498, European merchants could bypass the disputed waters of the Mediterranean and the dangers of traveling through Muslim countries, and Alexandria suffered.

If the City Were Not So Ruined, 1558
Peregrino Brocardo

Beyond the Pepper Gate, . . . in a somewhat elevated location, stands Pompey's Pillar, of marvellous size: nothing similar or larger have I seen in Rome or anywhere else; and it is all the more impressive because it is undamaged, save for the leaves of the Corinthian capital which have been somewhat eroded by time and weather. . . . The streets of the city are very straight in all directions; and if the city were not so ruined, it would be a majestic sight.

Taking from Alexandria to Build Cairo, 1577
Filippo Pigafetta

The walls of Alexandria are all built not of bricks but of square-cut stone, and these stone blocks were part of the old buildings of Alexandria. . . . In another street, parallel to the one in which I said the church of St Mark stands, you can see the wonderful temple adorned with various beautiful columns, which, in Christian times, was the seat of the Patriarchate, built as a square, open in the middle. Now it is the chief Mosque of Alexandria. . . . An astonishing thing about Alexandria is that the whole city is hollow beneath (except for the foundations of the major buildings which stand on earth), and stands over vaults and on columns; and in the vaults and wells water is stored. . . . In the people's dwellings you can see many pieces of marble and stone of different colours, cut in squares, circles, star and other shapes which, with exceptional skill, the good people of ancient times employed to cover the floors and the walls of their houses; a really wonderful work as much for the shaping and fitting together of those well-cut stones as for their quality and excellence, and the diversity of their colours; there are some houses there in which such construction remains intact and you can admire the mastery of the work in the floors and walls. That art is now completely lost, and no one is able to make new things, but they are so much valued that people gather up the pieces and transport them from place to place, and I myself have seen that in one old house they had taken up a most beautiful floor and transported it to Cairo to be used in a new house. Nowadays all the beautiful things of Alexandria are moved to Cairo, and of late you can see so many of these works both in the houses and in the mosques, Cairo having increased so much in grandeur through the ruination of Alexandria.

Heat and Decay, 1612
William Lithgow

Alexandria is the second Port in all Turky: It was of old a most renowned City, and was built by Alexander the great, but now is greatly decayed, as may appeare by the huge ruines therein: It hath two havens, the one whereof is strongly fortified with two Castles, which defend both it selfe and also Porto vecchio : The fields about the Towne are sandy, which ingender an infectious ayre, especially in the moneth of August, and is the reason why strangers fall into bloody fluxes and other heavy sicknesses. . . .

This Citty is mightily impoverished since the Trading of Spices that were brought through the red Sea, to Ægypt, and so over Land to Alexandria & its Sea-port: Whence the Venetian dispersed them over all Christendome; but are now brought home by the backe-side of Affricke, by the Portugals, English, and Flemings, which maketh both Venice, and Alexandria fare the worse, for

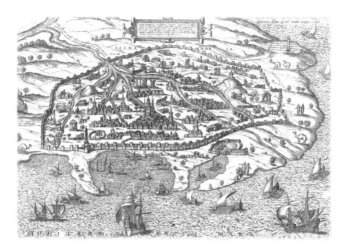

want of their former Trafficke, and commerce in these Southerne parts: whence Venice grew the mother nurse to all Europe for these Commodities, but now altogether spoyled thereof, and decayed by our Westerne Adventures, in a longer course for these Indian soyles.

This Citty was a place of great Merchandize, and in the Nycen Councell was ordayned to be one of the foure Patriarchall seas; the other three are Antiochia, Jerusalem, and Constantinople. Heere in Alexandria was that famous Library which Ptolomeus Philadelphus filled with

700,000 volumes: It was he that also caused the 72 Interpreters to translate the Bible: Over against Alexandria, is the little Ile Pharos, in the which for the commodity of Saylers the aforesaid King builded a watch-towre of white Marble; being of so marvellous a height, that it was accounted one of the seven wonders of the world. . . .

Expecting fifteene dayes heere in Alexandria for passage, great was the heate the French men and I indured, in so much that in the day time, we did nought but in a low roome, besprinckle the water upon our selves, and all the night lye on the top or platforme of the house, to have the ayre; where at last bidding good-night to our Greekish Host, we imbarked in a Slavonian shippe, belonging to Ragusa; and so set our faces North for Christendome.

Tracing Strabo amid the Ruins of Alexandria, 1737
Richard Pococke

As we approached [Alexandria] we had a very agreeable prospect: of the famous column, of the walls of the old city, of the country covered with palm-trees, which grow to a great height, rising up above the buildings of the city. And on the twenty-ninth we arrived in the port of Alexandria, after a very pleasant and agreeable voyage of twenty-three days. . . .

The famous Pharos, or light-house, was on a rock at the east end of the island, that was on every side encompass'd with water, and so in a manner a small separate island, which seems to be the spot on which the castle is built, at the entrance of the new Port; and the pillars seen in a calm sea within the entrance may be the remains of that superb building: These pillars I saw when I went out in a boat on a calm day, and could see to the bottom. My observing so nicely, and so near the castle, was much taken notice of; and, as I was inform'd, several soldiers, who were that day on guard in the castle, were punish'd for permitting me to examine the port so exactly. . . .

The first thing I did at Alexandria was to pace round the walls, and take the bearings; which I did with so much caution, that I thought I could only have been observed by the Janizary that attended me; not withstanding it was soon publickly reported about the town, that I had measured the city walls by palms. . . .

The palace, with the suburbs belonging to it, was a fourth part of the city; within its district was the Museum, or Academy, and the burial place of the Kings, where the body of Alexander was deposited in a coffin of gold, which being taken away, it was put into one of glass, in which condition, it is probable, Augustus took a view of the corpse of that great hero, and with the utmost veneration scatter'd flowers over it, and adorn'd it with a golden crown. As the Mahometans have a great regard for the memory of Alexander, so there have been travellers, who relate, that they pretended to have his body in some mosque; but at present they have no account of it. When Alexandria was no longer the residence of Kings, it is very natural to think that their palace in time fell to ruin, and that the materials of it were removed to the part of the city that was inhabited, and probably also to build the inner walls; tho' along by the sea there are still great remains, and on the shoar are seen several pieces of porphyry, and other fine marbles, where the antient palace stood. . . . .

The street which extended the whole length of the city, from the gate of Necropolis to the gate of Canopus, is said to have been one hundred feet wide, and, doubt-less, had in it many magnificent buildings, as appears from the granite pillars still remaining in two or three parts. Among them was the Gymnasium, or publick schools, to which there were Porticos in extent above half a quarter of a mile; it might be where there are great ruins to the west of that street, and several large red granite pillars standing. The Forum, or court of judicature, was also probably another building in this magnificent street, and might be where some pillars remain nearer the sea. . . .

Among the remains of Alexandria, the most extraordinary are those cisterns which were built under their houses, supported by two or three stories of arches on columns, in order to receive the Nile water by the canal, as they do at this day. . . .

The great lake Mareotis, which was formerly navigable, is now generally dry, and has only water in it for some time after great rains: it is probable the canals which convey'd the water to it from the Nile, have been obstructed. . . . The canal of Canopus, which brings the water to Alexandria, would likewise be stopped up, if they were not sometimes at great expence in cleaning it, which was done when I was in Egypt, and the water continued in it two months longer than it did before it was cleansed. . . .

Cleopatra Would Be Lost in Her Own City, 1768
James Bruce

The 20th of June, early in the morning, we had a distant prospect of Alexandria rising from the sea. Was not the fate of that city perfectly known, a traveller in search of antiquities in architecture would think here was a field for long study and employment. It is in this point of view the town appears most to the advantage. The mixture of old monuments, such as the Column of Pompey, with the high moorish towers and steeples, raise our expectations of the consequence of the ruins we are to find. But the moment we are in the port the illusion ends, and we distinguish the immense Herculean works of ancient times, now few in number, from the ill-imagined, ill-constructed, and imperfect buildings, of the several barbarous masters of Alexandria in later ages. . . .

It is in vain then to expect a plan of the city, or try to trace here the Macedonian mantle of Dinocrates; the very vestiges of ancient ruins are covered, many yards deep, by rubbish, the remnant of the devastations of later times. Cleopatra, were She to return to life again, would scarcely know where her palace was Situated, in this her own capital. There is nothing beautiful or pleasant in the present Alexandria, but a handsome street of modern houses, where a very active and intelligent number of merchants live upon the miserable remnants of that trade, which made its glory in the first times.

A Sentimental Tourist, 1779

Eliza Fay

23rd July, a.m. We are now off Alexandria, which makes a fine appearance from the sea on a near approach; but being built on low ground, is, as the seamen say "very difficult to hit." We were two days almost abreast of the Town. There is a handsome Pharos or light-house in the new harbour, and it is in all respects far preferable; but no vessels belonging to Christians can anchor there, so we were forced to go into the old one, of which however we escaped the dangers, if any exist. . . .

24th July. Having mounted our asses, the use of horses being forbidden to any but Musselmans, we sallied forth preceded by a Janizary, with his drawn sword, about three miles over a sandy desert, to see Pompey's Pillar, esteemed to be the finest column in the World. This Pillar which is exceedingly lofty, but I have no means of ascertaining its exact height, is composed of three blocks of Granite (the pedestal, shaft, and capital each containing one). When we consider the immense weight of the granite, the raising of such masses appears beyond the

powers of man. Although quite unadorned, the propor-
tions are so exquisite, that it must strike every beholder
with a kind of awe, which softens into melancholy when
one reflects that the renowned Hero, whose name it
bears, was treacherously murdered on this very Coast,
by the boatmen who were conveying him to Alexandria.
His wretched wife stood on the vessel he had just left,
watching his departure, as we may very naturally suppose, with inexpressible anxiety. What must have been
her agonies at the dreadful event! Though this splendid
memorial bears the name of Pompey, it is by many supposed to have been erected in memory of the triumph
gained over him at the battle of Pharsalia. Leaving more
learned heads than mine to settle this disputed point, let
us proceed to ancient Alexandria, about a league from
the modern town, which presents to the eye an instruc-
tive lesson on the instability of all sublunary objects. This
once magnificent City, built by the most famous of all
Conquerors, and adorned with the most exquisite productions of art, is now little more than a heap of Ruins,
yet the form of the streets can be still discerned. . . .

We also saw the *outside* of St. Athanasius' Church, who was Bishop of this Diocese, but, it being now a Mosque, we were forbidden to enter, unless on condition of turning Mahometans, or losing our lives, neither of which alternatives exactly suited my ideas, so that I deemed it prudent to repress my curiosity. I could not, however, resist a desire to visit the Palace of Cleopatra, of which few vestiges remain. The marble walls of the Banqueting room are yet standing, but the roof is long since decayed. Never do I remember being so affected by a like object. I stood in the midst of the ruins, meditating on the awful scene, till I could have almost fancied I beheld its former mistress, revelling in luxury, with her infatuated lover, Mark Anthony, who for her sake lost all. . . .

I forgot to mention that Mr Brandy met us near Cleopatra's Needles, which are two immense obelisks of Granite. One of them time has levelled to the ground; the other is intire. They are both covered with hieroglyphic figures, which, on the sides not exposed to the wind and sand from the desert, remain uninjured; but their key being lost, no one can decipher their meaning. I thought

Mr B— might perhaps have heard something relative to them; he however, seems to know no more than ourselves. A droll circumstance occurred on our return. He is a stout man of a very athletic make, and above six feet high; so you may judge what a curious figure he must have made, riding on an ass, and with difficulty holding up his long legs to suit the size of the animal; which watched an opportunity of walking away from between them, and left the poor Consul standing, erect, like a Colossus: in truth, it was a most ludicrous scene to behold.

With Napoleon at the Capture of Alexandria, 1798
Vivant Denon

When the shadows of the evening delineated the outline of the city; when I could distinguish on our approach the two ports; the thick walls, flanked by a great number of towers, which at present contain nothing but hillocks of

sand, and a few gardens, in which the pale green hue of the palm-trees scarcely tempers the burning whiteness of the soil; the Turkish fortress, the mosques, their minarets or towers, and the celebrated pillar of Pompey, my imagination recurred to past ages. I saw art triumph over nature, and the genius of Alexander employ the active medium of commerce, to lay on a barren soil the foundations of a superb city, which he selected to be the depositary of the trophies of the conquest of the universe. . . .

It would be impossible for me to describe what I felt on landing at Alexandria, where there was no one to receive us, or to prevent our going on shore. We could scarcely prevail on a group of beggars, leaning on their crutches, to point out to us the head-quarters. All the houses were shut: those who had not dared to fight had fled; and those who had not been killed in the combat, had concealed themselves, for fear of being put to death, according to the oriental custom. Every thing was new to our sensations; the soil, the form of the buildings, the persons, customs, and language of the inhabitants. The first prospect which presented itself to our view, was an extensive burying-ground, covered with innumerable tomb-stones of white marble, on a white soil. Among these monuments were seen wandering several meagre women, with long tattered garments, resembling so many ghosts. The silence was only interrupted by the screeching of the kites which hovered over this sanctuary of death. We passed from thence into narrow and deserted streets. . . .

During the whole of my progress through this long and melancholy city, Europe and its gaiety were brought to my recollection only by the chirping and activity of the sparrows. . . .

On the 4th, in the morning, I accompanied the commander in chief [Napoleon], who visited the forts, that is to say, a collection of clumsy buildings in a ruinous state, in which worn-out guns relied on stones that served them for carriages. The general's orders were to demolish whatever was unserviceable, and to repair only what might be useful, to prevent the approach of the Bedouins. He paid particular attention to the batteries for the defence of the harbours.

We passed near Pompey's pillar. This monument is in the predicament of almost every thing famous, which loses on a near scrutiny. . . .

Subterraneous researches made on this spot might also ascertain the site of the city in the time of the Ptolomies, when its commerce and splendour changed its original plan, and rendered it immense. That of the caliphs, which still exists, was but a diminution of the ancient city, notwithstanding it comprehends within itself, at this time, plains and deserts. This circumvallation being built of ruins, the edifices bring unceasingly to the remembrance destruction and ravage. The jambs and lintels of the doors of the dwelling-houses and fortresses consist entirely of columns of granite, which the workmen have not taken the pains to shape to the use to which they have applied them. They appear to have been left there merely with a view to attest the grandeur and magnificence of the buildings, the ruins of which they are. In other places a great number of columns have been applied to the construction of the walls, to support and level them; and these columns, having resisted the ravages of time, now resemble batteries. In short, these Arabian and Turkish buildings, the productions of the necessities of war, display a confusion of epochs, and of various industries, more striking and more approximated examples of which are no where else to be found. The Turks, more especially, adding absurdity to profanation, have not only blended with the granite, bricks and calcareous stones, but even logs and planks; and from these different elements, which have so little analogy to each other and are so strangely united, have presented a monstrous assemblage of the splendour of human industry, and its degradation. . . .

We came afterwards to the obelisk, named Cleopatra's needle: another obelisk thrown down at its side, indicates that both of them formerly decorated one of the entrances of the palace of the Ptolomies, the ruins of which are still to be seen at some distance from thence. . . .

An inspection into the present state of these obelisks, and the fissures which existed at the time even when they were fixed on this spot, prove that they were merely fragments at that period, and that they had been brought from

Memphis, or from upper Egypt. They might be conveyed to France without difficulty, and would there become a trophy of conquest, and a very characteristic one, as they are in themselves a monument, and as the hieroglyphics with which they are covered render them preferable to Pompey's pillar, which is merely a column, somewhat larger indeed than is everywhere to be found. . . .

The greater part of the divisions, after they were landed, had merely passed through Alexandria to encamp in the desert. I was also under the necessity of quitting this city, a place of great importance in history, where the monuments of every epoch, and the wrecks of the arts of so many nations, are heaped together confusedly; and where the ravages of wars, ages, and of a humid climate, impregnated with sea-salt, have been productive of greater changes, and have wrought more mischief than in any other part of Egypt.

Alexandria Refounded
by Muhammad Ali

In 1805 Muhammad Ali, an Ottoman adventurer of uncertain ethnic background from what is now northern Greece, made himself master of Egypt and forced the sultan in

Constantinople to recognize him as governor (pasha). Playing on his Macedonian origins, Muhammad Ali fostered the association between himself and Alexander the Great. An admirer of the West, he devoted his energies to modernizing Egypt, encouraging European immigration, capital, and expertise, and he established a dynasty, his successors bearing the title of khedive and then of king. By the time of his death in 1849 he had transformed Egypt into a secure destination for tourists who now came to Alexandria determined to see what little there was left to see.

The Rebirth of Alexandria under Mohammed Ali, 1885
Baedeker's Handbook for Travellers

During the middle ages Alexandria sank into insignificance. Its commerce received a deathblow by the discovery of the sea-route to India round the Cape of Good Hope, and the discovery of America entailed new losses. After the conquest of Egypt by the Turks (in 1517) the city languished under the infamous regime of the Mamelukes, the harbours became choked with sand, the population, which had once numbered half a million souls, dwindled down to 5000, and the environs were converted into a sterile and marshy wilderness. . . .

The decay of the once powerful seaport was at length effectually arrested by the vigorous hand of Mohammed Ali, who improved the harbours and constructed several canals. The chief benefit he conferred on Alexandria was the construction of the Mahmudiyeh Canal, which was so named after the reigning [Ottoman] Sultan Mahmud. By means of this channel fresh water was conducted to the town from the Rosetta branch of the Nile, the adjoining fields were irrigated anew, and Alexandria was again connected with the Nile and the rest of Egypt, the products of which had long found their only outlets through the Rosetta and Damietta mouths of the river. The enterprising pasha began the work in 1819, employing no fewer than 250,000 labourers, and completed it at a cost of 7½ million francs. He also improved the whole canal-system of the Delta, the works being chiefly superintended by the aged and eminent Linant de Belleville-Pasha, general director of public works, and other French engineers.

The Rapid Growth of Alexandria, 1847
Murray's Handbook to Egypt

Plague, and the Turkish system of Government, have lessened and still continue to lessen, the population of all Egypt, Alexandria alone excepted; which through increasing commerce, contains nearly ten times the number of inhabitants it had before the time of Mohammed Ali.

Foreigners Welcomed, 1872
François Levernay

In 1790, Alexandria was no more than a poor village of between 5000 and 6000 inhabitants. Mohamed Ali, by lifting the ban which prohibited Christian ships from entering the Old Port, by warmly welcoming the foreigners and generously paying for the many different services these latter rendered to Egypt, saw the growth in this country and, principally, at Alexandria of a large colony coming from all regions of the civilised world and soon the city of Ptolemy, once fallen into neglect, was to awaken, new, grand and prosperous.

The British Consul Writes of his Arrival, 1816
Henry Salt

My reception here has been very gratifying. Colonel Misset and Mr Lee, the Levant Company's consul, had prepared everything in the pleasantest way for my comfort, and all the foreign consuls stationed here have vied in paying me every possible attention. In a few days, as soon as I have arranged the business of the Consulate with Colonel Misset, I shall proceed to Cairo, where the Pasha [Mohammed Ali] at present resides, though it is said that in a short time he proposes to come down to Alexandria to spend the summer, for which purpose he has lately built a magnificent house, on the point where formerly stood the Plague Hospital. If this should prove true, I shall at the same time return to Alexandria, at least, if I can procure any place to put my head in, as just now the town is so crowded with Europeans that it is not possible to hire a house of any kind, or even rooms for a temporary occupation. . . . .

The trade of Egypt, or rather the Pasha's monopoly, goes on in a very flourishing way. There are not less than an hundred ships in harbour, and more than a third of them under English colours, the greater part of which are waiting for cargoes of grain. The first harvest has been very abundant, and the season is promising for the ensuing crops. The Pasha has made so many alterations in Alexandria that it is scarcely to be recognized for the same place. He has very absurdly, in my opinion, repaired, or rebuilt, the whole line of the old walls, which in consequence have become, instead of picturesque ruins, a regular and ugly mass of modern fortifications, very neatly *chunam'd* it is true, but too weak, and far too extensive, to prove of the slightest use in case of a siege. The same misfortune has likewise befallen the old Pharos, which is now completely modernized, and would make a becoming object only for the bottom of a citizen's garden. . . . .

To add strength to this judicious plan of fortification, the Pasha is now engaged in the Herculean task of levelling the hills outside of the walls. Some hundreds of poor devils of Arabs and buffaloes are engaged in this wise undertaking, which are watched in their labours by a pretty large detachment of troops; yet still, as might be expected, they advance very slowly, in their operations, removing heaps of rubbish from place to place without any System, and thus reducing one hill only to form another.

I had entertained a hope, on first hearing of this scheme, that some good might result from laying bare the antiquities concealed under these masses of ruins, but, in examining what they have already done, there appears little hope of any valuable discovery resulting from their labours, as they seem to content themselves with merely breaking up the surface, and this they pulverise so completely with the rude machines employed on the occasion, that it must be something very hard indeed which can resist being broken to pieces by their clumsiness. . . .

I shall contrive to look after their progress in levelling as much as the plague will permit, but, unfortunately, this malady appears at present to be gaining ground both here and at Cairo.

The Works and Delights of Mohammed Ali, c.1822
John Carne

After a delay of a few hours we landed at Alexandria. It was mid-day; the heat was excessive, and there were few passengers in the streets. We were quickly doomed to feel what might well be termed the succession of the Egyptian plague; swarms of flies were perpetually fastening on our faces and eyes, so that we could scarcely find our way, and were obliged to keep our handkerchiefs perpetually waving. When we entered a coffee-house, our sherbet or lemonade was instantly covered by a dark mass of insects, if we happened to leave up the tin cover with which the drinking-vessels are always provided to guard against this invasion. We went to an okkal, and ordered some dinner: the apartment was filled with a variety of people of different costumes: a Turk felt disposed to entertain them with a song—he put his two fore-fingers behind his ears, and bending forward as he sat cross-legged, ejected such hideous nasal sounds, intended to be pathetic, that we were obliged to take refuge in a small room upstairs. Here they soon brought us a dish of kid, deliciously dressed, and a dessert of fruit, which, with some excellent coffee, made a superb repast after the starvation on board ship. We hired apartments in a private house, and took possession of

them the same evening; but the mosquitoes were dread-
fully annoying—it was almost useless to close your eyes,
for you were quickly awakened by half-a-dozen keen
bites on different parts of the body; but the face was the
favourite part, which next morning looked any thing
but pale or fair. . . .

[Mohammed Ali] is very fond of Europeans, and has
engaged a great many in his service; and being perfectly free
from bigotry to the faith of the Prophet, he never requires
them to change their religion. He is ardently desirous to
improve his country, and has established a sugar-manufac-
tory on the Nile, and several of cotton in Cairo.

He longed for the luxury of eating ice; and there
being no such thing in Egypt, Mr Salt, the British
Consul-general, sent to England for an apparatus for
making it. The machine was conveyed, on its arrival,
to the Pacha's palace, and the Nile water made use of
for the purpose. Mohammed Ali hung over the whole
operation with intense curiosity; and when, after several
disappointments, a large piece of real ice was produced,
he took it eagerly in his hand, and danced round the

room for joy like a child, and then ran into the harem to show it to his wives and mistresses; and ever since he luxuriates upon it.

The great canal of Cleopatra, which he has lately made, or rather revived, forty miles in length, connecting the Nile with the sea at Alexandria, is an extraordinary work: for a considerable time he employed a hundred and fifty thousand men about it, chiefly Arabs of Upper Egypt; of these, twenty thousand died during the progress of the work.

Alexandria Built Upon Its Past, 1836
Sarah Haight

In every direction are to be seen the tops of columns projecting from the ground, belonging to some Christian church or pagan temple buried beneath. Within a few days one of these has been entirely excavated, and proves to be of the Roman era. Underneath the city are vaults and arches, so that the entire city may have stood on pillars. These vaults were cemented and used as cisterns to contain the waters of the Nile, which once a year, at its

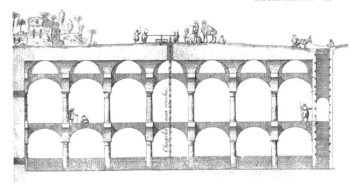

greatest height, was conducted hither by a canal. These vast reservoirs served for the rest of the year to supply the wants of a population of many hundreds of thousands, not only for ordinary family use, but for their innumerable private baths; besides which, there were three thousand public baths in constant use.

The well-shafts through which the water was drawn up in the public streets are still found at the corners, and used by the present inhabitants. In the ruins of private houses are to be seen the circular marble curbs, worn into deep channels by the action of the bucket ropes. This immense volume of water, after precipitating its particles of earth and other foreign matter brought down by the

Nile, remains sweet, pure, and delightfully cool during the long and intense heats of summer. . . .

Besides the pacha, there are numerous private speculators who are continually turning over the accumulated rubbish of this vast field of ruin, in search merely of the most ordinary materials for building. All that had much value has long since disappeared, though occasionally some granite and marble columns are thrown out. The hotel at which we are staying was lately a villa belonging to an English merchant in the city. All the materials for the house and high garden wall were excavated on the premises. Fragments of columns, capitals, and friezes are fancifully worked into the garden walls and facade of the house. There is scarcely an acre of ground that will not furnish sufficient materials from far beneath the surface to build a large mansion.

Seeing the Sights, 1842
Sophia Poole

To tell you of our landing, of the various and violent contentions of the Arab boatmen for the conveyance of our party, of our really polite reception at the custom-house,

and of our thankfulness when enjoying the quiet of our
hotel, would be to detain you from subjects far more
interesting; but I long to describe the people by whom we
were surrounded, and the noisy crowded streets and lanes
through which we passed. The streets, until we arrived at
the part of the town inhabited by Franks, were so narrow
that it was extremely formidable to meet any thing on
our way. They are miserably close, and for the purpose of
shade, the inhabitants have in many cases thrown matting
from roof to roof, extending across the street, with here
and there a small aperture to admit light; but the edges
of these apertures are generally broken, and the torn
matting hanging down: in short, the whole appearance
is gloomy and wretched. I ought not, however, to com-
plain of the narrowness of the streets, for where the sun is
not excluded by matting, the deep shade produced by the
manner in which the houses are constructed, is most welcome in this sunny land; and, indeed, when we arrived at
the Frank part of the town, which is in appearance almost
European, and where a wide street and a fine open square,
form a singular contrast to the Arab part of the town, we

scarcely congratulated ourselves; for the heat was intense, and we hastened to our hotel, and gratefully enjoyed the breeze which played through the apartments. . . .

Mounds of rubbish and drifted sand occupy nearly the whole site of the ancient city. Within the area surrounded by the present wall, besides some monuments of the ancient city, are two convents and a synagogue, several groups of houses and huts, with a few walled gardens containing chiefly palm-trees. . . . It must have been an extensive city, but it is impossible to mark its precise limits. Certainly its remains alone convey an idea of its having been a flourishing town, and considerably more important than the Arab city which succeeded it. Desiring to see the obelisks before the heat of the day, we set out early, and having passed the great square, we entered the field of ruins, and found a number of peasants loitering among miserable huts, while a few children, in a state of nudity, and extremely unsightly in form, were standing or sitting in the entrances of their dwellings. . . . We saw little worthy of remark until we reached the obelisks, which are situated at an angle of the enclosure, almost close to the shore of the new harbour; I mean those obelisks called Cleopatra's Needles. . . . When the British army was in Alexandria in 1801, operations were commenced for transporting the fallen obelisk to England; but the commander-in-chief refusing to sanction the undertaking, it was abandoned, and nothing is said of its being resumed, although Mohammed Alee offered the monument to us some years ago. After viewing the obelisks, we thankfully turned homewards, for the sun had risen, and the heat became intense. . . .

The pillar called Pompey's is undoubtedly a magnificent monument. . . . The shaft is beautifully wrought, but sadly disfigured by numerous names inscribed in very large characters, with black paint. They have mostly been written by persons who have ascended to the summit. This they have contrived by flying a large paper kite, and causing it to descend so that the cord rested on the top of the capital; by these means, they succeeded in drawing a stout rope over it; and having accomplished this (to use the naval term) they easily "rigged shrouds," by which to ascend. This exploit has been performed several times, generally by naval officers, who have caused the name of their ship to be painted on the shaft. Among the adventurers, an English lady once ascended to the summit.

Indignities, 1845
W.M. Thackeray

The riding of a donkey is, after all, not a dignified occupation. A man resists the offer at first, somehow, as an indignity. How is that poor little, red-saddled, long-eared creature to carry you? Is there to be one for you, and another for your legs? Natives and Europeans, of all sizes, pass by, it is true, mounted upon the same contrivance. I waited until I got into a very private spot, where nobody could see me, and then ascended—why not say descended, at once?—on the poor little animal. Instead of being crushed at once, as perhaps the rider expected, it darted forward, quite briskly and cheerfully, at six or seven miles an hour; requiring no spur or admonitive to haste, except the shrieking of the little Egyptian gamin, who ran along by asinus's side. . . .

The curiosities of Alexandria are few, and easily seen. We went into the bazaars, which have a much more Eastern look than the European quarter, with its Anglo-Gallic-Italian inhabitants, and Babel-like civilisation. Here and there a large hotel, clumsy and whitewashed, with Oriental trellised windows, and a couple of slouching sentinels at the doors, in the ugliest composite uniform that ever was seen, was pointed out as the residence of some great officer of the Pasha's Court, or of one of the numerous children of the Egyptian Solomon. His Highness was in his own palace, and was consequently

not visible. He was in deep grief, and strict retire-
ment. It was at this time that the European newspapers
announced that he was about to resign his empire; but

the quidnuncs of Alexandria hinted that a love-affair, in which the old potentate had engaged with senile extravagance, and the effects of a potion of hachisch, or some deleterious drug, with which he was in the habit of intoxicating himself, had brought on that languor and desperate weariness of life and governing, into which the venerable Prince was plunged. Before three days were over, however, the fit had left him, and he determined to live and reign a little longer. A very few days afterwards several of our party were presented to him at Cairo, and found the great Egyptian ruler perfectly convalescent.

This, and the Opera, and the quarrels of the two prime donne, and the beauty of one of them, formed the chief subjects of conversation; and I had this important news in the shop of a certain barber in the town, who conveyed it in a language composed of French, Spanish, and Italian, and with a volubility quite worthy of a barber of *Gil Blas*.

Then we went to see the famous obelisk presented by Mehemet Ali to the British Government, who have not shown a particular alacrity to accept this ponderous present. The huge shaft lies on the ground, prostrate, and desecrated by all sorts of abominations. Children were sprawling about, attracted by the dirt there. Arabs, negroes, and donkey-boys were passing, quite indifferent, by the fallen monster of a stone—as indifferent as the British Government, who don't care for recording the glorious termination of their Egyptian campaign of 1801. If our country takes the compliment so coolly, surely it would be disloyal upon our parts to be more enthusiastic. I wish they would offer the Trafalgar Square Pillar [Nelson's Column] to the Egyptians; and that both of the huge ugly monsters were lying in the dirt there side by side.

Pompey's Pillar is by no means so big as the Charing Cross [Trafalgar Square] trophy. This venerable column has not escaped ill-treatment either. Numberless ships' companies, travelling cockneys, &c., have affixed their rude marks upon it. Some daring ruffian even painted the name of "Warren's blacking" upon it, effacing other inscriptions—one, Wilkinson says, of "the second Psammetichus." I regret deeply, my dear friend, that I cannot give you this document respecting a lamented monarch, in whose history I know you take such an interest. . . .

We went the round of the coffee-houses in the evening, both the polite European places of resort, where you get ices and the French papers, and those in the town, where Greeks, Turks, and general company resort, to sit upon uncomfortable chairs, and drink wretched muddy coffee, and to listen to two or three miserable musicians, who keep up a variation of howling for hours together.

Nothing to See, 1846
Harriet Martineau

Before our anchor was down, we had a crowd of boats about us, containing a few European gentlemen and a multitude of screaming Arabs. I know no din to be compared to it but that of a frog concert in a Carolina swamp. We had before wondered how our landing was to be accomplished . . . . But we had help. An English merchant of Alexandria kindly took charge of us; put our luggage into one boat and ourselves into another, and accompanied us ashore. The silence of our little passage from the ship to the quay was a welcome respite: but on the quay we found ourselves among a crowd of men in a variety of odd dresses, and boys pushing their little donkeys in among us, and carts pulled hither and thither—everybody vociferating and hustling in the starlight. Our luggage was piled upon a long cart, and we followed it on foot: but there was an immediate stoppage about some custom-house difficulty—got over we know not how. Then the horse ran away, broke his girths, and scattered some of our goods. At last, however, we achieved the walk to our hotel—a walk through streets not narrow for an eastern city. All the way we had glimpses of smoking householders in their dim interiors, turbaned artisans, and yellow lamplight behind latticed windows. The heat was oppressive to us, after our cool days at sea. The rest of the evening was fatiguing enough. . . .

When I looked out of my window early the next morning, I saw, at the moment, nothing peculiarly African. The Frank Square is spacious, and the houses large; but they would be considered shabby and ugly anywhere else. The consular flag-staves on the roofs strike the eye; and the flood of brilliant sun-light from behind the minaret made the morning as little like England in November as could well be. Presently, however, a string of camels passed through the square, pacing noiselessly along. I thought them then, as I think them now, after a long acquaintance with them, the least agreeable brutes I know. Nothing can be uglier, unless it be the ostrich; which is ludicrously like the camel, in form, gait and expression of face. The patience of the camel, so celebrated in books, is what I never had the pleasure of seeing. So impatient a beast I do not know—growling, groaning and fretting whenever asked to do or bear anything, looking on such occasions as if it longed to bite, if only it dared. . . .

When the camels had passed, some women entered the square from different openings. I was surprised to see their faces hardly covered. They pulled their bit of blue rag over, or half over, their faces when any one approached them, as a matter of form; but in Alexandria, at least, we could generally get a sight of any face we had a mind to see; excepting, of course, those of mounted ladies. As we went up the country, we found the women more and more closely veiled, to the borders of Nubia, where we were again favored with a sight of the female countenance. The next sight in the square was a hareem, going out for a ride—a procession of ladies on asses—each lady enveloped in a sort of balloon of black silk, and astride on her ass—her feet displaying a pair of bright yellow morocco boots. Each ass was attended by a running footman; and the officer of the hareem brought up the rear. . . .

We had a better view than this, one morning, from the fort on Mont Cretin. I believe it is the best point for a survey of the whole district; and our thinking so seemed to give some alarm to the Arabs, who ceased their work to peep at us from behind the ridges, and watch what we did with telescope, map and compass. The whole prospect was bounded by water—by the sea and Lake Mareotis— except a little space to the north-east; and that was hidden by an intervening minaret and cluster of houses. Except where some palms arose between us and Lake Mareotis to the south, and where the clustered houses of the town stood up white and clear against the morning sky, there was nothing around us but a hillocky waste, more dreary than the desert, because the dreariness here is not natural but induced. If we could have stood on this spot no longer ago than the times of the Ptolemies (a date which we soon learned to consider somewhat modern) it would have been more difficult to conceive of the present desolation of the scene than it now is to imagine the city in the days of its grandeur. On the one hand, we should have seen, between us and the lake, the circus, with the multitude going to and fro; and on the other, the peopled gymnasia. Where Pompey's Pillar now stands alone, we should have seen the long lines of the colonnades of the magnificent Serapeum. On the margin of the Old Port, we should then have seen the towers of the noble causeway, the Heptastadium, which connected the island of the Pharos with the mainland. The Great Harbor, now called the New Port, lay afar this day, without a ship or boat within its circuit; and there was nothing but hillocks of bare sand round that bay where there was once a throng of buildings and of people. Thereabouts stood the temple of Arsinoe, and the theatre, and the inner palaces; and there was the market. But now, look where we would, we saw no sign of life but the Arabs at work on the fortifications, and a figure or two in a cemetery near. The work of fortification itself seems absurd, judging by the eye; for there appears nothing to take, and therefore nothing to defend. Except in the direction of the small and poor-looking town, the area within the new walls appears to contain little but dusty spaces and heaps of rubbish, with a few lines of sordid huts, and clumps of palms set down in the midst; and a hot cemetery or two, with its crumbling tombs. I have seen many desolate-looking places, in one country or another; but there is nothing like Alexandria, as seen from a height, for utter dreariness.

The Joyful Eastern Sun, 1849
Florence Nightingale

19 November 1849:

The Pharos and masts of Alexandria, and Pompey's pillar, and a long low line of coast now appeared against the crimson clouds, and from his own Morgenland, his own East, the sun sprang up as he ought to do. I cannot describe the initiation into old poetry he gives you on his first rising in the East. He does not come up slowly and solemnly, and rather sadly, as he does in the chill dawn in England, while one is feeling a sinking, and a trembling, and a shivering from having been up in the cold to see him; but he leaps from the horizon into the sky, whips his fiery steeds, shouts for joy, and brings in brilliant day immediately; it is his "glad" course here, and the flood he pours forth is "living" light. One never understood the word "living" before. It is as if each ray was a messenger, alive. The northern sunlight is like lamplight. I shall never forget my first sight of him. . . .

You cannot conceive, besides, the impatience to get on shore after eight nights on shipboard, in a crowded steamboat, with an atmosphere of, I really believe, 120° in our cabin, the men drinking punch from morning till night, the women giggling and clacking.

Before nine we had landed, and were on our way to the Frank square, in the omnibus, for it was already too hot to walk. Before ten, Mr Gilbert had called upon us in our inn-yard, and he has already placed a janissary at our disposition (who does everything for us), and given us everything we could want.

The first thing after we had saved our baggage from the hurrying Indians, was to ask our janissary, Alee, who walks before us, and is the most gentle, yet most dignified being I ever saw (I am quite afraid to speak to him), to show us the way to the baths. After a longish walk we came to a gateway, and through an avenue of date-palms, bananas, and petunias, trellised overhead, to a long, low building with Pompeian baths, in red, and green, and blue squares, and with low archways (against the heat), leading from one to the other. Egyptians sitting about at their dinner of fruits. They gave us a tangle of palm-tendrils to wash ourselves with, with a lump of beautiful Egyptian soap in the middle of the nest: all European appliances are vile compared to those palm-tendrils. . . .

Of course there are drawbacks to all this light and beauty; the mosquitoes are at this moment (six o'clock in the morning) so bad, that I am surrounded by the dead bodies of those slain in single combat. The heavy dew drove us home last night before sunset. But what is that to pay for the joy of the East? . . .

24 November 1849:

Yesterday we took our first donkey ride to the catacombs; but donkey riding in Egypt is a very different
thing from donkey riding elsewhere. The donkey is very
small, and you are very large (the Egyptian is a very tall
race), and you sit upon his tail; and as he holds his head
very high, you look like a balance to his head. After
mounting, a feat which is effected by curling your right
leg round your saddle bow (the saddles are men's), you
set off full gallop, running over everything in your way;
and the merry little thing runs and runs and runs like
a velocipede. There is nothing in Alexandria but the
Frank Square, which is larger than any square in London, and the huts of the Alexandrians, which look more
like a vast settlement of white ants than anything else.
The hut is always but one room, about eight or nine
feet square (the walls prolonged in front to make a sort
of alcove), about six feet high, made of plastered white
mud, with or without windows, which are furnished
with shutters; no chimney; nothing inside but one pot,
and sometimes a box. They seldom adjoin; but a space

is left between each. The first effect is that of a vast collection of ovens. You can hardly believe they are human dwellings. Some, I should think, were altogether but a cube of five feet. . . .

One day we drove to the site of the battle of Aboukir, a dreary plain of white sand covered with white stones; a scanty fringe of palm trees in the distance; the broken wall of Nicopolis, built by Augustus, in the foreground, a road, many inches deep in sand, through which we waded: it looked like the shroud of an empire's body, the ghastly tale of a kingdom's whitening bones. I went down to the sea shore, not being able to bear the abomination of desolation, and walked along the beach, where the breakers were rolling and tossing in, and the sun was setting exactly behind the Pharos of Alexandria, in all the triumphal march of an Eastern sunset, with the green transparent caves of the sea beyond, not like the funeral pomp of that white winding sheet behind, but like a patriot hero going home, full of light and love.

Americans on Tour, 1867
Mark Twain

When we reached the pier we found an army of Egyptian boys with donkeys no larger than themselves, waiting for passengers—for donkeys are the omnibuses of Egypt. We preferred to walk, but we could not have our own way. The boys crowded about us, clamored around us, and slewed their donkeys exactly across our path, no matter which way we turned. They were good-natured rascals, and so were the donkeys. We mounted, and the boys ran behind us and kept the donkeys in a furious gallop, as is the fashion at Damascus. I believe I would rather ride a donkey than any beast in the world. He goes briskly, he puts on no airs, he is docile, though opinionated. Satan himself could not scare him, and he is convenient—very convenient. When you are tired riding you can rest your feet on the ground and let him gallop from under you.

We found the hotel and secured rooms, and were happy to know that the Prince of Wales had stopped there once. They had it every where on signs. No other princes had stopped there since, till Jack and I came.

We went abroad through the town, then, and found it a city of huge commercial buildings, and broad, handsome streets brilliant with gas-light. By night it was a sort of reminiscence of Paris. But finally Jack found an ice-cream saloon, and that closed investigations for that evening. The weather was very hot, it had been many a day since Jack had seen ice-cream, and so it was useless to talk of leaving the saloon till it shut up. . . .

In the morning the lost tribes of America came ashore and infested the hotels and took possession of all the donkeys and other open barouches that offered. They went in picturesque procession to the American Consul's; to the great gardens; to Cleopatra's Needles; to Pompey's Pillar; to the palace of the Viceroy of Egypt; to the Nile; to the superb groves of date-palms. One of our most inveterate relic-hunters had his hammer with him, and tried to break a fragment off the upright Needle and could not do it; he tried the prostrate one and failed; he borrowed a heavy sledge hammer from a mason and tried again. He tried Pompey's Pillar, and this baffled him. Scattered all about the mighty monolith were sphinxes of noble countenance, carved out of Egyptian granite as hard as blue steel, and whose shapely features the wear of five thousand years had failed to mark or mar. The relic-hunter battered at these persistently, and sweated profusely over his work. He might as well have attempted to deface the moon. They regarded him serenely with the stately smile they had worn so long, and which seemed to say, "Peck away, poor insect; we were not made to fear such as you; in ten-score dragging ages we have seen more of your kind than there are sands at your feet: have they left a blemish upon us?"

Multitudes of Ships, 1868
Reverend A.C. Smith

The novelty of the scene rivetted our attention, and kept most of us in open-mouthed astonishment and admiration. Vessels of all sizes and shapes thronged the harbour, but we had no eyes for ships—their crews occupied all our attention. Arabs, Egyptians, Nubians, Syrians, Turks, Greeks, with swarthy skins and flowing robes—and all apparently screaming, at the top of their voices, the most unintelligible jargon—formed such a scene of indescribable novelty, confusion, and noise, as positively paralysed all our attempts to prepare for disembarking, and held us fixed in a long stare of amazement and wonder. I defy any European mind, however well regulated, to be prepared for this first view of Eastern life. Let a man be never so well read in Oriental travels; have drank never so deeply of the stores of information as to its habits and customs; have realised as far as possible all the imagery of the Arabian Nights, and other glowing pictures of Eastern scenes—still the reality will so far surpass all his previous conceptions, as literally to take away his breath, when he comes into personal contact with Eastern life for the first time. Now, the harbour of Alexandria is perhaps better calculated than any other spot in the world for this introduction to Oriental scenes; and as the European traveller steams into it, and threads the long lanes of vessels which always congregate therein, a new world seems to open to his astonished eyes and ears, and he stands amazed at the sight. At least that was our experience: there were such multitudes of ships, of every build and of every rig, the elegant lateen-sail of the Levant of course prevailing;

sailors in every imaginable costume, the universal fez (or *tarboosh*) and the full trousers of the East of course predominating; and such a hubbub and very Babel of tongues, screeched at the highest pitch of which the human voice is capable, Arabic of course in the ascendant: these sounds and sights absorbed our whole attention, and kept us thoroughly occupied till we were fairly landed on the quay.

The Unreal City, 1883
R. Talbot Kelly

My first introduction to Egypt was in 1883, and was ushered in in rather a startling manner. We were still two or three hours' steaming distance before land could possibly be in sight, when suddenly we saw, inverted in the sky, a perfect miragic reproduction of Alexandria, in which Pharos Light, Ras-el-Tin Palace, and other prominent features were easily distinguishable. The illusion continued for a considerable time, and eventually as suddenly disappeared, when, an hour or two later, the real city slowly appeared above the horizon! A good augury, surely, of the wonders I hoped to discover on landing!

Modern Cosmopolitan Alexandria

Alexandria came of age in 1890 when it established the Municipality and became the first self-governing city in the Middle East, a city remarkable for the way in which people of different national and cultural backgrounds lived side by side in harmony.

City of Tolerance and Respect, 1922
Evaristo Breccia

What had become of the noisy city where "no one was idle," where artists, poets, philosophers and critics had exercised their refined intelligence, where the love of gain was equalled only by the love of pleasure, and where women were as beautiful as they were frail?

Nothing remained! The sadness of death was everywhere. The area of the town shrunk more and more, and the cemeteries, which originally were situated to the East and West, encroached upon and almost entirely usurped the land formerly crowded by habitations.

Here and there stood a solitary palm tree, its leafy crest, high above its long naked trunk, floating mournfully in the northern breeze. Cleopatra's Needle and Pompey's Pillar, in melancholy pride, like two giants surviving the disaster, gazed at one another from afar and told each other a tale of sorrow.

Slowly but surely the sand, in the idle and abandoned harbour, was silting up the sheltering ports that had held the mighty fleets of the Hellenistic epoch.

To the great Mohamed Ali belongs the credit of resuscitating the dead town of Alexandria. Success rapidly followed his courageous initiative. The remodelling of the Mahmudia Canal in 1819, together with the works undertaken in the harbour of Eunostos, helped Alexandria to recover part of the commercial activity which had been so prominent a feature of her former life. The Prince offered safe and liberal hospitality to Europeans, and their trading colonies grew in number very quickly. Death gave way to life. . . .

Nothing is more false than the widely spread idea that Alexandria has nothing to show to its visitors. This fiction has arisen from the fact that Alexandria is owing to its position, a point of arrival and a point of departure. The tourist arrives in Egypt eager to see the Pyramids and the grand ruins of Pharaonic civilisation whose description have stirred his imagination since childhood. When he returns, he is homesick or anxious to see other countries. Alexandria, for him, is nothing but a port. But if he does not tarry, he will have but an incomplete idea of the marvellous history of this country, dead a hundred times and a hundred times resuscitated, and he will leave with a regrettable gap in the series of his impressions and his knowledge. . . .

One might be inclined to believe that such a variety of races, languages, religions and manners could not constitute a town whose essential qualities are precisely tolerance and reciprocal respect. Alexandria, however, is a proof that much prejudice and racial hatred, much chauvinism, much religious fanaticism may grow milder, and may even disappear, when a race or a nationality has occasion to live in daily contact with other races and other nationalities. . . . Each retains his political, social and moral ideal, but they all respect that of others, and no one insists that his is the best or the finest and that it ought to govern the world.

The Graeco-Roman Museum, 1891
Constantine Cavafy

Certainly the fine initiative of the citizens of Alexandria will contribute greatly to the enrichment of the Museum. It is worth recommending, however, that excavations in sections of the city be undertaken especially where discoveries of antiquities seem certain, whenever they do not interfere too greatly. The ground on which we live undoubtedly hides many artifacts and many relics of ancient Alexandria.

The Alexandrian Museum is full of interest for all the friends of antiquity and learning, but especially for us Greeks. It is rather like a treasury of familiar objects. It speaks to our imagination regarding the glorious Hellenism of Alexandria. It presents to us an image of that noble civilisation that developed so robustly in Egypt, as in another Greece, which injected into the Orient the Greek spirit and bequeathed Greek refinement and grace to the Oriental ideas with which it came into contact.

Under Alexandria's Spell, 1905
Ronald Storrs

Alexandria is not an obvious city; she requires, before revealing her self, time, study and love. I liked her well, from the Sharia Sharif Pasha, which has something of the brilliant narrowness of Bond Street, to the sinister rowdiness of the Anastassi, the Gumruk Quarter and the Attarin Caracol. Under the spell of this Egyptian atmosphere I began to confess myself *anima naturaliter Levantina* of the Levant of Pharaoh, Solomon, Homer, Alexander, Virgil, St Paul, Dante and Dandolo, *Antony and Cleopatra* and *The Merchant of Venice*; a world that may look back, rather than forward like the Great Continents, but which between Homer and the Sermon on the Mount the "clear fountain of eternal day" has given us that whereby we live, move and have our being.

My life was physically hard and unsparing. I had leased for three pounds a month the coastguard cottage on the eastern promontory of Stanley Bay in Ramleh, half surrounded by the sea and never silent from the roaring of the waves, and had there a few books and a small piano; but I was seldom in it. I had become (for the sake of the free stall) operatic critic to *The Egyptian Gazette* and thus absorbed by nightly draughts at the gracious little Zizinia Theatre the unexacting modes and measures of *La Boheme*, *Tosca*, *Thais* and *Lohengrin*, the severest form of Wagner then acceptable south of Naples, though *La Valeria* and *Maestri Canton di Norimberga* were soon to follow. It was something of an effort after ten minutes' walk to the tram

into Alexandria, twenty-five minutes' journey and then twenty minutes' walk to the Customs, to return home after duty, change and attend the Opera, write the critique on some marble-topped table, post it, catch the 1.30 a.m. tram the last from Alexandria, and catch it again outwards after some four hours' sleep, for next day's work.

Carnival, early 1900s
Count Patrice de Zogheb

Carnival time could not pass unnoticed in our cosmopolitan town and the last days before Lent were enlivened by several days of rejoicing and masquerading in the streets, houses and places of public entertainment. There was a procession of carnival cars full of gay beauties with masks and dominos romping through the streets. In the evening, there would be a *veglione* or masked ball, usually in favour of some charity or other, at the Opera house and revelling would go on till dawn all over the town.

Venice with Mosques, 1910
Douglas Sladen

Alexandria is an Italian city: its vegetation is almost Italian; it has wild flowers. Its climate is almost Italian; it has wind and rain as well as fierce blue skies. Its streets are almost entirely Italian; and Italian is its staple language. Even its ruins are Roman. If it was not for the mosque of Kait Bey, where the Pharos ought to be, and a few minarets in the strip of old Alexandria between the two forts, you would not believe that you were in a city of Islam. I never was in such a rebuilt place. When Mehemet Ali a century ago determined to restore Alexandria, so that his name might be coupled with Alexander the Great's, the city had dwindled down to a village of 5000 inhabitants.

The cutting of the Mahmudiya Canal made Alexandria the Nile seaport, instead of Rosetta and Damietta. They have no commerce now. To-day Alexandria is a city of 350,000 inhabitants, and the accommodation for them all had to be built. A few of the classical ruins are showing, most of the rest lie undisturbed under the mounds between Alexandria and Aboukir. Another Rome may await their investigator. Alexandria consists therefore of history and unhistorical buildings. . . .

Another watery attraction of Alexandria is the old Mahmudiya Canal. It is not really old; it was only constructed by Mehemet Ali, but it looks as old as the Bahr Yusuf, which the Egyptians say was cut by the Joseph of the Book of Genesis, while the banks and the villas which adorn them have obviously seen better days. If Egyptians could only leave well alone this would be an attraction. The cafes hanging over the waters have some of the picturesqueness of the tea-houses of Japan, while the decaying villas give the effect of one of those delightful back-canals of Venice, which have palaces with gardens, if Venice only had mosques. Unfortunately, Alexandria is

a commercial city, and the Mahmudiya Canal gives, as it was designed to give, water carriage. So many an old villa has given way to a modern factory, though the factories, to do them justice, look as if they would soon enter into the general scheme of decay. You seldom see one human being at work in them. As yet the old palm-gardens, mostly in the process of destruction, and the gyassas, crawling or beached along the canal, with tall brown wings or spidery masts and yards, keep the Mahmudiya a picture, especially when the sunset is pouring through the stately sycamore avenue of the city bank. I have even seen a pasha's dahabeah on it, and there are charming seats round the spreading trees in belvederes over the water, commanding views of the great Lake Mareotis. . . .

We saw some really delightful lake scenery, and a great collection of dust-heaps, which looked as if they had been evolved from a sulphur mine, but really contain ancient Alexandria, whenever the funds and energy are forthcoming to excavate it. This will never be till they want the earth to make another mole, or to turn more of the eastern harbour into a garden suburb. . . .

Flowers by the Seashore, 1914
Edith Louisa Butcher

Towards the west of Alexandria, beyond the stone-quarries of Mex, the flowers grow thickly and are larger in size. Here are the purple bells of the grape-hyacinth, and the pale lilac of a kind of sea-lavender. One may gather about forty varieties in a morning's walk, but it is very difficult to learn the names of most of them. Here, too, straight out of the sand, by the blue ripples of the sea, grows one of the most beautiful wild-flowers of Egypt—the white amaryllis. Its delicate white flowers seem almost as much

out of place by the seashore as a lady in white satin building sand-castles, and yet this is so truly its home that the
commonest name for it is the Mex lily.

Bedouins of Ramleh, 1902
Baedeker's Egypt

As in the time of Herodotus, the tent of the Beduin is
still his home. Where it is pitched is a matter of indif-
ference to him, if only the pegs, which secure it are
firmly driven into the earth, if it shelter his wife and
child from the burning sunshine and the chilly night-air,

and if pasturage-ground and a spring be within reach. At Ramleh on the coast, near Alexandria, the traveller will have an opportunity of seeing a whole colony of the poorest class encamped in their tents, where they live in the most frugal possible manner, with a few miserable goats and the fowls which subsist on the rubbish in their neighbourhood.

Though professors of El-Islam, they are considerably less strict in their observances than the fellahin of the valley of the Nile, who are themselves sufficiently lax, and above all they sadly neglect the religious duty of cleanliness. They do not observe the practice of praying five times a day, and they are as a rule but slightly acquainted with the Koran. Relics of their old star-worship can still be traced among their customs.

Ramleh, 1872
François Levernay

A few years ago Ramleh (sand) well deserved its name as there was nothing but bare sand dunes. At first, the fresh air which one can breathe there attracted certain merchants; the example was rapidly followed and today, thanks to the facility of travel accorded by a railway, it has become fashionable to spend summer in the countryside; the population in the summer months is around 6500 and 3200 in winter.

Ramleh in the Early Days, 1935
Mabel Caillard

Ramleh lies abut five miles to the east of Alexandria, near the site of that Nikopolis where Strabo, some two thousand years earlier, saw "buildings fronting the sea not less than a city." Climate and erosion have played havoc with the remains of ancient Alexandria: Pompey's Pillar—which is really Diocletian's, and thus a monument to the topsy-turvydom which is one of Egypt's most enduring fascinations—stands alone to recall its former glories. Of its once splendid suburb nothing was left by the time that we arrived upon the scene but a little temple on a ledge of the cliffs, fast crumbling to ruin, some broken columns and traces of cisterns and catacombs along the shore, and the foundations of houses that had long since slipped into the sea, and of which the outlines were still clearly visible, on calm days, beneath the limpid water.

The place we found was less pretentious, but with a peculiar charm of its own. Some sixty or seventy houses were scattered over the sand according to the will and fancy of their owners, only linked by the common inter-est of the little railways that maintained communication with the town. There were no other roads: one followed a camel track, or struck a beeline across the desert, that in winter was firm and fresh-smelling from the rain and sprinkled with exquisite small wild flowers in count-less variety. The Bedouins brought then their primitive ploughs and sowed their grain between one habitation and the next, and in March a blaze of poppies and yellow daisies shared the furrows with the springing corn. ...

In the absence of roads, donkeys were the accepted mode of transport and groups of them, with their attendant donkey-boys, were to be seen at each station on the Ramleh line, awaiting the arrival of the trains from town. They were sturdy little beasts, up to any weight; my father required an especially tall one, as he was himself over six feet in height; and even so, by riding without stirrups, he avoided the unpleasant shock when one fell—as Egyptian donkeys have a nasty trick of doing—under him. He simply stood up and walked over his head. . . .

At last some narrow roads began to appear in the configuration of Ramleh, as it developed on a roughly symmetrical plan. They were mere sandy tracks until Mr Alderson bethought him of the old refuse mounds of broken pottery around Alexandria, and threw down a few camel loads of the stuff in front of his house. This excellent example was generally imitated and fragments of ancient Greek and Roman vases were thumped into the roads, producing a practicable surface and a most pleasant appearance. It was, indeed, a sorry day when those terra cotta lanes gave way to macadam, presaging the change from the old Ramleh, peaceful and picturesque, to the magnificent and vulgar place into which it has finally grown. . . .

There was a spell about that tideless, sapphire sea, its sands wreathed with lovely shells and fringed by flat rocks and shining pools, in which you might sometimes find a nautilus, or a living octopus that would suddenly coil its long tentacle about a prodding walking-stick and snap it in half before you had time to draw it away. You lingered to watch the sunset from the top of the low cliff, in springtime clothed with the satin sheen of mauve ground-stock that filled the evening air with its evanescent perfume. You faced the gale on mornings of wild storm to see the mountainous waves rolling in or breaking over the rocks, and the water-spouts forming along the inky horizon. Once a seagull fell, with a wing broken by the wind, in our garden; it was soon so tame that it would join the procession to the dining-room at meal-times and limp round the table begging for food.

'Was' is the word I have used in writing of the Ramleh sea; and indeed, though it is still blue, and calm or rough as the wind blows, its charm is no longer the same. The view of it to-day is obscured by blocks of flats on the cliff's edge; the beaches are civilised and crowded, controlled—more or less—by the Municipality and the police.

Alexandrian Civilization, 1917

E.M. Forster

The civilisations of Egypt are, roughly speaking, three in number. There is Egypt of the Pharaohs which still moves tourists and popular novelists, but which means nothing to the resident, nothing at all. Then there is Arab Egypt in which we more or less live and less or more have our being—a real civilisation this, but static and incomprehensible. And thirdly, there is Egypt of the Levant—the coastal strip on which since the days of Herodotus European influences have rained. A European personally, I feel kindly towards this coastal strip. It raises my interest and even a sense of romance. It is so small in area yet first and last it has produced so much that is good. It always has been and always must be a civilisation of eclecticisms and of exiles. But despite these defects it has managed to carry on century after century, buried at times by the sands of the south, yet always reappearing. There is a certain little bird—I forget its name but its destiny is to accompany the rhinoceros about and to perform for him various duties that he is too unwieldy to perform for himself. Well, coastal Egypt is just such a little bird, perched lively and alert upon the hide of that huge pachyderm Africa. It may not be an eagle or a swan. But unlike the rhinoceros its host it can flit through the blue air. And now and then it sings.

The Eastern Harbour Corniche, 1917
E.M. Forster

What Forster here calls the New Quay, later known as the Eastern Harbour Corniche, was built in 1906. In the 1930s the corniche road was extended along Alexandria's coastline as far east as the royal palace at Montazah, nearly twenty miles distant from Fort Kait Bey.

It is interesting when a great public work fails to touch the popular imagination. Were our citizen asked what is the most remarkable object in the district he would reply, "Pompey's Pillar," or more cheerfully, "The Cosmograph" [a cinema], and never give a thought to the curve of stone behind him. Many public works are rightly

ignored, because they are silly or brutal; it is right that an eternal vacuum should surround the Albert Memorial in London or fill the Piazza Vittoria Emmanuele at Florence. But the New Quay is so fine, while historically it is the successor of the old Ptolemies' causeway that once divided the two harbours. It does not deserve obscurity. Seen from the south, when there is mist in the morning, its beauty is fairy like; seen from the northern extremity it forms a complete ring round a circle of blue water. . . . To stretch right and left in an exquisite parabola and attain poetry through mathematics—that is its only aim, and an aim not unbecoming to the city of Eratosthenes, and Euclid.

Royalty, 1926

Judge Jasper Brinton

Down to Sidi Gaber to see the King [Fuad] off for Cairo. The same old ceremony, but, as always, elegant and snappy, with plenty of military display. The Cabinet was there and the usual long double line of pretty much everybody. The King's train backs in from the palace and he gets off at one end of the platform and walks down the Royal Alley Way shaking hands. I stood behind, but he spotted me and we said "How do you do" as usual. I felt a little apologetic, as I did not call on him at either end of this year's holiday. However, if I had thought of it, I would have gone just to see his new rooms at Ras el Tin Palace. He is a well-dressed dapper fellow, with an agreeable manner, and quite accomplished in the superficial arts, at least, of being a king. He can afford to do things up in style and people seem to like it, although he is about as far as a king could be from any contact with his people. It offered an occasion to sell my piano to our Consul for thirty-five Egyptian pounds. Delighted to do this, as I need the pounds and don't need the piano.

View from His Balcony, 1920s
Constantine Cavafy

Where could I live better? Below, the brothel caters for the flesh. And there is the church which forgives sin. And there is the hospital where we die.

From the same balcony Constantine Cavafy looked out upon his city and listened to its music.

The God Abandons Antony
Constantine Cavafy

When at the hour of midnight
an invisible choir is suddenly heard passing
with exquisite music, with voices—
Do not lament your fortune that at last subsides,
your life's work that has failed, your schemes that have
    proved illusions.
But like a man prepared, like a brave man,
bid farewell to her, to Alexandria who is departing.
Above all, do not delude yourself, do not say that it is a
    dream,

that your ear was mistaken.

Do not condescend to such empty hopes.

Like a man for long prepared, like a brave man,

like to the man who was worthy of such a city,

go to the window firmly,

and listen with emotion,

but not with the prayers and complaints of the coward

(Ah! supreme rapture!)

listen to the notes, to the exquisite instruments of the
   mystic choir,

and bid farewell to her, to Alexandria whom you are
   losing.

Cotton Brokers, 1937
C.S. Jarvis

The backbone of the population of Alexandria are the cotton brokers, who neither grow cotton nor manufacture it. They must break it, whatever that may mean, but it is obviously the best thing to do with cotton as the poor fellow who grows it has to live on 7½*d* a day and the man who manufactures it goes bankrupt every other year; but the Alexandrian, who breaks it, attends cocktail parties every evening of his life.

Cotton Frenzy, 1918
Mabel Caillard

The cotton boom at the end of the war … was a boom that excelled all precedent in magnitude and Alexandria, with her gambler's heart, went mad with excitement. One heard of immense fortunes being made on the Bourse; of others already established rocking perilously near the margin of safety; and of the usual failures, whose protagonists were washed up, a few days afterwards, by the sea into which they had thrown themselves in their despair. But the sobering effect of these tragedies upon the survivors soon gave way to the stimulus of a fresh rise in prices and more mad bids for fortune. Men besieged their banks or their brokers with urgent requests for loans or last-minute instructions; women sold their jewels for one last throw of the winning die. The very serving-maids brought out their hard-earned savings and obstructed the pavements outside the Exchange to place their purchases of cotton-seed cake, which started at a lower figure than the real article and thus provided a gamble within the reach of all.

Rivalry between Alexandria and Cairo, 1937
C.S. Jarvis

Alexandria is very jealous of Cairo and is always training tennis and golf players to go and collect cups from the capital, and if Cairo has a riot in the streets Alexandria always has a bigger and better one next day; there seems to be more building going on in Alexandria and

therefore a better supply of bricks and stones to throw at the police. Also Alexandria has more Greek grocers to be looted and beaten.

At the Movies, 1937
Josie Brinton

Yesterday evening we went to see *Romeo and Juliet.* The movie house is amazing. The picture of course is in English but down at the bottom the conversation is shown in French and then they have a small screen on the side of the main one on which the conversation is shown in Greek and Arabic. Doesn't that sound cosmopolitan?

Alexandria
in the Second World War

In a few sudden months in 1940 the whole of the Atlantic coast of Europe had fallen into German and Italian hands and much of North Africa too. America was neutral and the Soviet Union had signed a non-aggression

pact with Germany, so that Britain stood alone against the fascist menace. Egypt was of critical strategic importance in this great conflict: Britain's Mediterranean Fleet was based at Alexandria, while Alamein, the last defensive position against the fascist advance, lay less than seventy miles west of the city. Fortunately for Alexandria it was the British fleet, not the city, that was the target of Axis air raid attacks and these were confined almost entirely to the Western Harbor. Meanwhile life in Alexandria effervesced and seemed unreal.

Air Raids on the Western Harbour, 1941
Judge Jasper Brinton

One of the most exciting civilian war jobs was the Volunteer Inshore Patrol—an auxiliary naval service organised by a few yachting enthusiasts at the request of the British Commander-in-Chief to protect the fleet lying in Alexandria harbour.

Among other forms of attack to which it was exposed were parachute mines dropped into the harbour and remaining unmarked. A nightly patrol curtain was accordingly established to be on watch from dusk until daylight, both inside and outside the harbour. Owners of private craft were invited to contribute their use and a corps of volunteer spotters were recruited. Headquarters of the patrol was the British Boat Club, with its charming old boat house inside the customs area, with a lawn sloping down to the water. Vi Goodchild, our Number One yachtswoman, undertook to keep the roster and check on the volunteer crews. At first we had only two boats inside the harbour and two outside. Each of us took our turn—once a week. Sometimes the outside patrol was a distinctly choppy business. The boats were supposed to be accommodated with "sleeping accommodation and facilities for cooking" but neither of these were very much in evidence. The crew brought their own snack and when off watch no one wanted to miss the interesting sights and sounds accompanying a night in the harbour. The whole enterprise was conducted with a high standard of efficiency. It was also very much of a lark.

The harbour itself was crowded and full of interest. Early in the evening the balloon barrage would go up—twenty or thirty balloons attached by wire to windlasses. Further protection was offered by the magnificent barrage of anti-aircraft guns which also encircled the harbour. One boarded one's boat and proceeded under sail to the assigned anchorage and spent the night keeping a careful watch for possible mines or other devices.

The situation was always dramatic but for the most part a scene of peace and quiet unless by good luck (from the watcher's standpoint), he found himself on duty during an air raid. A dozen searchlights would at once begin to search the skies for the approaching airplane. Generally, it was discovered, whereupon the anti-aircraft guns went into action. The noise was terrific. It was said to surpass the noise of the raids on London. It was all a fascinating sight. One could follow the shells, the flaming onions of the Bofors guns upwards towards a target which alas they never seemed to hit. On the other hand the enemy planes were kept at such a height that an effective raid was impossible. During the entire three years not a single naval unit was hit. In fact I don't recall a single plane that received a hit in the air.

Shorts at the Yacht Club, 1943
Noël Coward

September 17th

Bathed in the morning with Glynne and then we went with Penny and Mr and Mrs Finney to lunch at the Yacht Club. Now the Yacht Club in Alexandria is select and exclusive to an alarming degree although I suspect that the bulk of the members have little or no connection with

yachting. There were a number of elderly, mauve-looking ladies sitting on the terrace when we arrived. They were thickly coated with rice powder and were hissing sibilantly. We ordered cocktails and were then immediately asked to leave by the management because we were dressed in shorts and shirts. This was startling as it seemed to me that our attire was eminently suited both to the climate and the setting. Mr Finney, a usually influential man, remonstrated in vain and, in order to prevent the whole incident from developing into an unseemly brawl, we swept out with as much dignity as we could muster. This dignity was briefly disrupted by an ardent young man asking me for my autograph. Feeling myself to be on the horns of a dreadful social dilemma I asked the manager if it was contravening the club rules to sign autographs in shorts and if it was should I take them off? But he looked at me stonily and didn't reply.

We had a delicious lunch in the town and comforted ourselves with the reflection that as long as the Alexandria Yacht Club maintained its high moral standards, the war for freedom and civilisation really was worth winning.

The Dream-City Alexandria, 1942
Lawrence Durrell

Once the first sense of estrangement is over, the mind finds its surcease in the discovery of the dream-city Alexandria which underpins, underlays the rather commonplace little Mediterranean seaport which it seems, to the uninitiated, to be. It plays even today a somewhat unwilling role as a second capital for Egypt, the only relief offered a resident of Cairo—that burning-glass of a city, wedged between its deserts. It opens upon a dreaming sea and its Homeric waves are rolled and unrolled by the fresh breezes from Rhodes and the Aegean. Going ashore in Alexandria is like walking the plank for instantly you feel, not only the plangently Greek city rising before you, but its backcloth of deserts stretching away into the heart of Africa. It is a place for dramatic partings, irrevocable decisions, last thoughts; everyone feels pushed to the extreme, to the end of his bent. People become monks or nuns or voluptuaries or solitaries without a word of warning. As many people simply disappear as overtly die here. The city does nothing. You hear nothing but the noise of the sea and the echoes of an extraordinary history.

Sightseeing in Wartime Alexandria, 1943
Schindler's Guide to Alexandria

The Corniche.—Alexandria is a clean looking modern city with beautiful natural harbours. Man has striven to enhance nature's natural beauty by every possible means. The attractive arc of the central promenade is lined with lofty white buildings, with a green square here and there to dispel any monotonous effect. The magnificent Corniche has a fine wide tarmac surface along its entire 30 kilometres length. It is possible to drive with ease along the whole length enjoying all the while an uninterrupted view of the bay. This Corniche is claimed to be the finest and longest sea front drive in any town in the world—a justly deserved title.

Apart from motoring along the Corniche, an excellent impression of the city can be gained by taking a tram, some of which are double deckers, and afford a unique opportunity for sightseeing. . . .

The layout of the town is simple; Alexandria by its very closeness to the desert must cling to the coastline. The town only feebly penetrates for more than a few miles into the desert at any point.

Having realised this, one is apt to ask, "Where can I go—must I make perpetual promenades along the Corniche?" It certainly does appear so when looking at a map, but there are many places of interest to be seen just off the beaten track.

Descent into the Catacombs, 1944
Gwyn Williams

There are strange and lovely things still remaining from the Ptolemaic past, things which are often neglected by visitors hot foot for the Pyramids, pharaonic gold and the monstrous temples of Upper Egypt. This was a city committed to Alexander's hellenisation of the lands he conquered, by coming to terms with local ways and beliefs. The Macedonian Ptolemy, to be known as Ptolemy Soter, inherited Egypt when Alexander the Great died. Alexandria became the capital of his empire, which eventually took in Cyrene, Cyprus, Palestine and parts of Asia Minor as well as Egypt. From the beginning therefore Alexandria was not a part of Egypt but a city from which Egypt was governed. To symbolise this special arrangement, and to please both the Egyptians and Greeks he ruled over, Ptolemy invented a new god, a new religion. He took elements from the ancient Egyptian gods, the bull Apis, worshipped at Memphis, and Osiris, the sun-god and the greatest of them all, and blended their names into that of the new god, Serapis . . . . Sometimes he carries a formalised basket on his head to show that he was a harvest god and he always wears a benign expression. . . .

The temple area of the Serapeum has been cleared and excavated and there heads and figures of Serapis were found. Found there also was the life-size figure of the bull

Apis, in polished black granite, one of the most splendid animal sculptures ever made. Not far away, in a quarter called Kom-es-Shogafa, you may descend into the under-world of ancient Alexandria, the strangest catacombs I have seen. Here again there is a blend, but this is of the Roman era and is more grotesque than the subtler mixing of the Ptolemies. Guarding a door are two odd figures. One is Anubis, with a dog's head but dressed as a Roman soldier. On the other side is the crocodile god Sebek, but he also is kitted out with a Roman cloak and spear. . . .

These catacombs are altogether mysterious but there was one effect which particularly frightened me, and I observed this the first time I ever went down with someone else, so that I had someone to talk to. When I first spoke I had the eerie feeling that I could hear the echo of my voice a split second before I actually made the sound, and this happened every time I said anything. I suppose there must be some explanation for this but I can't think what it is. But if the *déjà vu* can be explained, why not the *déjà etendu*? Leueen McGrath came to Alexandria with the ENSA theatre group and, since this was one of my show pieces,

I took her down into the catacombs. On the way down the stone steps I was foolish enough to joke about Orpheus and Eurydice. She was impressed with the underworld but didn't feel well in this queer décor. I took her back to the villa, not to her hotel, since I felt responsible. She stretched out on the settee and passed out. I flapped around and fortunately she soon recovered and later seemed none the worse. Alexandria is a place where *l'eternel retour* is apt to catch you without warning, and the whole incident taught me not to stick my nose unnecessarily into a myth.

An Air Raid Alert, 1941
Josie Brinton

There's a permanent blackout now so no one goes out at night—it's too difficult driving—besides being afraid to be caught in a raid, and there are air raid alerts throughout the day. I went into town this morning to do some shopping and I parked the car and went into a shop to buy some material for a dress when—"woob-woob-woob"—the alarm sounded. The shop quickly shut its doors and everyone rushed off the streets and to the nearest shelters while a police car patrolled the streets with an amplifier saying "Prenez alerte—depechez-vous, depechez-vous"—terribly eerie. That alarm lasted 45 minutes and we won't know until tomorrow's paper what it was about. Anyway no bombs were dropped. One old lady in the shop had hysterics and another woman asked the shopkeeper if he played cards—saying we might as well play something.

Restaurants and Entertainments in Wartime Alexandria, 1943
Schindler's Guide to Alexandria

Dining Out

General.—It will be of interest for the newcomer to Alexandria to know something of the leading restaurants and cafés. This chapter cannot hope to cover even all the first-class establishments, some are noted for their quietness and select atmosphere, others for their gaiety and music, and others for French cooking and other specialities. Some of the leading restaurants also combine cabaret and dancing with their other services.

Union (Officers.)—The Union Restaurant in Old Bourse Street is much frequented by the English residents of Alexandria, who like its select atmosphere and quiet locality. It is well known as having one of the best kitchens in Egypt, specialising in high-class French cooking.

Pastroudis and Monseigneur.—Pastroudis, 39 Rue Fouad 1er is one amongst the best first-class restaurants in Alexandria. It is very well patronised by the élite of Alexandria society. The patisserie is one of the best in town, and prices are moderate. The Bar, with Reuters Ticker nearby, is the rendez-vous of preference in Alexandria.

The Monseigneur Dance Hall and Restaurant on the sea front, near Ramleh Tram Station, is under the same management. It is reserved for Officers and Civilians. On Saturdays and Sundays the well-known dance band is a great attraction, and a gay time is had by all in very select surroundings. …

Baudrot.—Baudrot in Rue Fouad 1er (opposite Cook's) is a very fashionable high class restaurant, with bar, tea-room, and pastry shop. It is very pleasant for afternoon teas. In the evenings private dances and receptions are frequently given in the large hall.

Athineos.—Athineos is one amongst the best restaurants in Alexandria. It is in a very central position on the Corniche, entrance being from the Ramleh Tram Station side. The Café overlooking the Eastern Harbour and Fort Kait Bey, is a very pleasant place to enjoy a drink or afternoon tea. In the evening two dancing sessions are held, one from 6.30 to 8.45 and the other from 10.00 to 11.15. On Sundays there is a light musical concert at 11 o'clock. The ventilation is perfect, the fresh sea air promoting an appetite which an aperitif from the excellent wine cellars puts on high mettle, and can only be satisfied by the perfectly served French cooking, for which this establishment is noted. The first class dinner is 35 piastres, and lunch PT 30, two meals which will be remembered long after the expense is forgotten. In the Patisserie, the succulent sweetmeats and pastries are kept in conditioned showcases, to ensure freshness. . . .

Grand Trianon.—Foremost in the French Café type establishments, the Grand Trianon stands in a class of its own. Occupying three sides of a block facing the sea on the one side, and Ramleh Square and Rue Zaghloul on the other sides, its position leaves little to be desired. Tables are arranged on the pavement, in the French Boulevard style, for those who wish to take their coffee and watch the street scene, at the same time getting the full benefit of the fresh sea breezes.

The interior is a work of art, one section alone, that containing the tempting sweetmeats and pastries, costing over LE 18,000 to decorate. The fine carvings were imported from Switzerland, and are worthy of close study. Great marble pillars adorn the majestic tea rooms and grill room, whilst beautiful Persian carpets muffle every footstep. The tasteful tables and chairs are also very fine, and were again imported from Switzerland. In the evenings, a dazzling spectacle is produced by the brightly lit chandeliers, and the polished silver tea services. Full luncheons or dinners are not catered for, but light meals of chicken and ham can be arranged.

The biggest feature is the patisserie, where the finest pastries and chocolates are on show in air conditioned show cases. More pastries and sweetmeats are sold daily than by any other patisserie in Egypt.

A high-class Cabaret Floor show for the benefit of the troops, is given free of charge every evening at 6 o'clock.

The Femina cabaret which adjoins, opens at 8pm for officers.

There is a bar in the Grand Trianon and one in the Femina, the drinks are of the highest quality, being from an original pre-war stock of imported whisky and wines.

Cabarets

Phaleron Cabaret, 26 Midan Zaghloul.—The Phaleron Cabaret is essentially a place for dancing and watching Cabaret, the restaurant aspect plays a minor role, although light meals and drinks are on sale.

The situation is particularly good, being only 150 yards from Ramleh Tram Station or 100 yards from the Cecil Hotel facing Zaghloul Square. The building lies back from the road, behind a screen of trees.

During the Great War it was famous as the leading Cabaret open to Officers.

The interior has been recently re-decorated, and has a pleasing appearance. Numerous large mirrors and an abundance of lights add to the gaiety of the scene.

About ten different artists present pretty dancing numbers every evening at 10pm. There is a complete change of programme every fortnight.

Excelsior Cabaret, Corniche Road, Mazarita (Near Ramleh Tram Station).—The Excelsior Cabaret is classed amongst the first in Alexandria. It is open to Officers and Civilians only. The atmosphere is particularly gay over the weekends when tea dances are held. The jazz band is full of life, and there are many other attractions. The kitchen is particularly worthy of mention.

Out on the Town, 1941
Robert Crisp

Unfortunately I was gravely restricted in my operations by the limitations of a lieutenant's pay and the high cost of after-sunset living. To a certain extent I was able to cope with this by a squeamish reluctance to indulge myself in the ultimate expenditure with the attractive but extravagant cabaret girls and hostesses who people the Alex night. Also I was able to work my passage, more or less, through my two favourite restaurants.

Going into the Excelsior one evening, in a purely amateur spirit of joie-de-vivre, I did a Zulu war-dance in an interval between cabaret turns. Thereafter, whenever I came in for supper the band would break into a tribal rhythm, inviting me to perform my primitive gyrations and stompings which might have intrigued a Zulu but which he would certainly have found unrecognisable.

At the Phaleron, peopled by attractive Greek call-girls, I once took over the microphone while the band was playing "Tristesse"—that Chopin adaptation which was at the height of its popularity about that time—and managed to sing it all the way through in English. This was, apparently, the first time any band in Egypt had heard the words and, again, I became a regular performer.

On my good nights, depending on the applause and tolerance of the audience in both restaurants, the managements would decline to present me with the dinner bill. On some nights I succeeded in making a bloody fool of myself.

Vera was a cabaret girl at the Excelsior. She did a dance in a Spanish costume. Not the clickety-clack, castanetted, whirling sort, but slow-moving and sensuous, in keeping with the full curves of her body and thighs and an immobile quality in features of considerable beauty.

A little desperate with frustration, and a little more tight than usual, I broke into her act one evening, not finding it over-difficult to match the music and her movements. She was furious, but allowed it to show only in her eyes which glowed at me from under the broad-brimmed Spanish hat like an angry cat cornered under a sideboard.

Fortunately, both band and audience co-operated and, with her acceptance of the situation, I saw interest and amusement replace the anger in her eyes. At the end the sufficient applause settled the incident in my favour. She came and sat at my table for the rest of the evening—for free.

After that she joined me almost automatically every time I went to the Excelsior. . . . Sometimes I danced with her; sometimes I did my Zulu war-dance; most of the time we just sat and I ate my Escalope Viennoise and we drank wine and she would go to change for her act and come back after it dressed in the clothes in which she went home.

I wondered when she would let me make love to her. I was sure she would eventually, but I was aware of the holding back, the strange lack of communication on the subject. I sensed right from the beginning that she wanted to establish a different relationship with me than the quick matching of bodies which, I suspected, was a part of her profession. I accepted the attitude unquestioningly, and concurred in it. For one thing, I found it intensely flattering. . . .

I don't know what her home language was. I doubt whether she knew herself. She could speak half-a-dozen European tongues and was fluently vituperative in Arabic. She was completely international in the way in which only a stateless person can be. There was a community of such girls who rotated around the Middle East and North Africa (they probably still do) performing their uninspired cabaret turns, drinking weak tea at the price of double whiskies, earning their living by entertaining men in a variety of ways. . . .

A few nights later I saw her again at the Excelsior. It was just as though nothing had happened. But something had happened. I couldn't tell her this would be the last night; that we were not likely to see each other, touch each other, ever again. In the gharrie going to her flat I kissed her for the last time. I knew that I would always think of that last, innocent contact. . . .

Winter Walks in Alexandria, 1943
Theodore Stephanides

Lawrence [Durrell] was transferred to Alexandria as head of the Alexandrian branch of the Intelligence and Information Department with an office and staff of his own. I was not able to see him again until 15 January 1943, when I stayed for a fortnight in Alexandria while 58 General Hospital was getting ready to move to Bengazi, which had been evacuated in the meanwhile by Rommel's forces after his defeat by Montgomery at El Alamein. Lawrence was in his element; he was now his own boss and he was able to make good use of his knowledge of Greek as, at that time, Alexandria still contained a numerous Greek population. I visited him several times at his office, a busy place with the walls well covered with anti-German political posters in several languages. . . .

On 19 December 1943, I was given a fortnight's sick-leave which I spent with Lawrence . . . in one of the pleasantest quarters of Alexandria, composed mostly of detached villas surrounded by flowering gardens. It was here that I spent one of the nicest Christmases I had ever enjoyed. By this time Lawrence knew all about Alexandria, and he showed me the sites of some of its ancient monuments, including that of the Library and the famous Pharos. It was very interesting to look at the places where these famous monuments had once been, but, alas!, no ruins even of them still existed.

One of our favourite walks, when Lawrence could spare the time from his work, was the long promenade along the sea front with the Mediterranean on one side and the long line of low clustered villas on the other. The weather, fortunately, was on the whole fine; but an icy north wind sometimes blew accompanied by sudden showers of rain. The Alexandria beach was studded with

ALEXANDRIA - SIDI-BISH BEACH

a number of small beach houses; some of them, however, were quite large and elaborate—almost as big as small villas with two, three or four rooms.

On several occasions I was rather surprised to see furniture standing out in the rain, until Lawrence explained to me that these beach houses belonged to the Alexandria Municipality which rented them out. If the rent was not paid up promptly, the lessee's furniture (the houses were let unfurnished) was just thrown out and the house rented to someone else, as there was always a big demand for them. Lawrence added that clerical errors were frequent and that you sometimes found your furniture thrown out even though you *had* paid your rent in time. Sometimes the same house was rented to two different people at once—with considerable dissatisfaction all round.

War Effort, 1944
Lawrence Durrell

I am in charge of a goodish sized office of war-propaganda here, trying to usher in the new washboard world which our demented peoples are trying "to forge in blood and iron." It's tiring work. However it's an office full of beautiful girls, and Alexandria is, after Hollywood, fuller of beautiful women than any place else. Incomparably more beautiful than Athens or Paris; the mixture Coptic, Jewish, Syrian, Egyptian, Moroccan, Spanish gives you slant dark eyes, olive freckled skin, hawk-lips and noses, and a temperament like a bomb. Sexual provender of quality, but the atmosphere is damp, hysterical, sandy, with the wind off the desert fanning everything to mania. Love, hashish and boys is the obvious solution to anyone stuck here for more than a few years. I am sharing a big flat with some nice people, and atop it I have a tower of my own from which the romantics can see Pompey's Pillar, Hadra Prison, and the wet reedy wastes of Lake Mareotis stretching away into the distance and blotting the sky.

This is the world of the desert Fathers and the wandering Jews; the country eaten away like the carious jawbone of a mummy. Alexandria is the only possible point in Egypt to live in because it has a harbour and opens onto a flat turpentine sealine—a way of escape.

Alexandria Egyptianized

*After the Second World War a combination of Egyptian
nationalism and international events had the effect of revers-
ing Mohammed Ali's policy; people who had helped build*

*Alexandria were driven from their homes and the city ceased
to be cosmopolitan any more.*

The Storm, 1949
Jean Cocteau

The storm is doing its worst, and as neither windows nor
doors ever close in Alexandria, our rooms appear to be
riding the wind, then they explode, and at night we feel
that at any moment we shall leave our moorings and go
out to sea in tatters.

The Alexandrians hang on to their scaffolding. There
is nowhere else to go. No open country, no place to flee
to. They live with their houses one above the other like
passengers on a ship, on which the different classes live
their separate lives, and even those in adjoining cabins do not speak to each other because of some feud or
unpleasantness.

The storm keeps us from leaving. A delayed departure
is always wretched. In theory we have already left and
our ghosts linger behind.

The Pension Miramar, 1967
Naguib Mahfouz

Alexandria. At last. Alexandria, Lady of the Dew. Bloom of white nimbus. Bosom of radiance, wet with sky-water. Core of nostalgia steeped in honey and tears. . . .

Alexandria, I am here.

On the fourth floor I ring the bell of the flat. The little judas opens, showing Mariana's face. Much changed, my dear! It's dark on the landing; she does not recognise me. Her white face and golden hair gleam in the light from a window open somewhere behind her.

"Pension Miramar?"

"Yes, monsieur?"

"Do you have any vacant rooms?"

The door opens. The bronze statue of the Madonna receives me. In the air of the place is a kind of fragrance that has haunted me.

We stand looking at each other. She is tall and slim, with her golden hair, and seems to be in good health, though her shoulders are a little bowed and the hair is obviously dyed. Veins show through the skin of her hands and forearms; there are tell-tale wrinkles at the corners of her mouth. You must be sixty-five at least, my dear. But there is still something of the old glamour left. I wonder if you'll remember me.

She looks me over. At first she examines me; then the blue eyes blink. Ah, you remember! And my self comes back to me.

"Oh! It's you."

"Madame."

We shake hands warmly—"Goodness me! Amer Bey! Monsieur Amer!"—and she laughs out loud with emotion (*the long feminine laugh of the fishwives of Anfushi!*) throwing all formality to the winds. Together we sit down on the ebony settee beneath the Madonna, our reflections gleaming on the front of a glassed bookcase that has always stood in this hall, if only as an ornament. I look round.

"The place hasn't changed a bit." . . .

"Why have you come here now? The season's over."

"I've come to stay. How long is it since I saw you last?"

"Since . . . since . . . did you say 'to stay'?" . . .

"I felt the call of my birthplace. Alexandria. And since I've no relations I've turned to the only friend the world has left me." . . .

We settle everything in a few minutes, including the obligatory breakfast. She proves as good a businesswoman as ever, notwithstanding sweet memories and all that. When I tell her I've left my luggage at the station, she laughs.

"You were not so sure you'd find Mariana. Now you'll stay here with me forever."

I look at my hand and think of the mummies in the Egyptian Museum. . . .

As she sits there under the statue of the Madonna, I look at her and say, "Helen in her prime would not have looked as marvellous!"

She laughs. "Before you arrived, I used to sit here all alone waiting for someone, anyone I knew, to come through the door, I was always in dread of . . . of getting one of my kidney attacks."

"I'm sorry. But where are your people?"

"They've gone, every one of them." She purses her lips, showing her wrinkles. "I couldn't leave—where should I go? I was born here. I've never even seen Athens. And after all, who'd want to nationalise a little *pension* like this?" . . .

"Egypt's your home. And there's no place like Alexandria."

The wind plays outside. The darkness steals up quietly. She rises, switches on two bulbs of the chandelier and returns to her seat.

"I was a lady," she says, "A lady in the full sense of the word."

"You're still a lady, Mariana." . . .

"Monsieur Amer, I don't know how you can say there's no place like Alexandria. It's all changed. The streets nowadays are infested with *canaille*."

"My dear, it had to be claimed by its people." I try to comfort her and she retorts sharply.

"But we created it."

The Sea Remains, 1977
Robin Fedden

The Hellenes even today have their rallying points. The sea remains. Alexandria lives on its beaches, and the first

attraction of the place is also its most intimate link with the past. Along the corniche a wave curls in a dozen sunlit bays, catches the light, spills and runs nimbly up the sand. Farther out white spray shoots over the reefs and falls into the safety of quiet blue water. When the Greeks first came they brought something of the lucent quality of the Aegean. This quality, a curious infusion of light in water, makes one always turn one's head in Alexandria towards the sea. As it holds Nelson's ships and the weed-covered blocks of stone that were once the Pharos, so one imagines the sea to hold in solution the whole past of the city. Deeply blue in calm summer and rustling at the edge of many bays, it seems tense with association, as though it could barely carry its heavy historical precipitate. In such a stillness Menelaus returning from Troy beached at the island of Pharos, and Pompey the Great, as he was rowed towards the Pelusiac shore, sensing his treacherous end, bowed his head deeper over the dialogue of Plato. On such a glazed sea, where the fishing-boats today slide almost windless into harbour, Cleopatra's barge put out to the stroke of silver oars that dipped to the music of a flute. Alexandrian waters that hissed under her prow still preserve the memory of such occasions.

City of Memory, 2004
Gaston Zananiri

Though Alexandria is two thousand years old, it's still Alexandria. There is something of the past which returns every moment.

The Writers

KARL BAEDEKER (1801–59) was a German publisher of highly detailed and authoritative travel guides to which he also lent his name as an author. The first edition of Baedeker's *Egypt* was published in 1878.

EVARISTO BRECCIA (1876–1967) was an Italian Egyp- tologist and director of the Greco-Roman Museum in Alexandria from 1904 to 1931. He was subsequently professor of Greek and Roman antiquities at the University of Pisa.

JUDGE JASPER BRINTON (1878–1973), born in Philadel- phia, was an American judge on Egypt's Mixed Tribunals and eventually its president, the highest legal position in the land. He was also president of the Royal Archaeological Society of Alexandria.

JOSIE BRINTON (1916–89), born in Memphis, Tennessee, was married to Jasper Brinton's son John, who worked for the Alexandrian publisher Whitehead Morris.

24   **PEREGRINO BROCARDO** (d. 1590) was an Italian painter, musician, traveler and priest from Liguria whose letters, drawings, and maps provide a seemingly accurate description of Egypt in his time.

32   **JAMES BRUCE** (1730–94) was a Scottish traveler who studied and carefully drew the ancient monuments of North Africa and the Middle East before traveling to Ethiopia, where he traced the origins of the Blue Nile.

89   **EDITH LOUISA BUTCHER** (1854–1933), born in Lincolnshire, is best known for *The Story of the Church in Egypt*, her book about the Copts, and *Things Seen in Egypt*, her observations on Egyptian life. She was married to the Anglican chaplain of All Saints in Cairo.

92, 102   **MABEL CAILLARD** (1876–1935) was born in England but came to live in Ramleh aged eleven when her father was appointed postmaster general of Egypt. A lively and curious person who knew a remarkable range of people, her *Lifetime in Egypt* is a fascinating account of change in a rapidly developing city.

JOHN CARNE (1789–1844) was born into a strict Methodist family in Penzance, Cornwall. Though he became a clergyman, he never officiated and instead traveled to the Holy Land, which marked the beginning of his journeys throughout the Levant, which he wrote about extensively.   *49*

CONSTANTINE CAVAFY (1863–1933) is considered one of the greatest poets of the twentieth century. Of Greek parentage, he was born and died in Alexandria, which he made the center of his imaginative world.   *82, 100*

JEAN COCTEAU (1889–1963) was a French avant garde novelist, poet, playwright, artist, and filmmaker.   *133*

ANTHONY DE COSSON (1883–1940), who was born in England, was director of the Desert Railways in Egypt. He was a noted member of the Royal Archaeological Society of Alexandria and explored the Lake Mareotis region for its ancient remains.   *15*

109   **NOËL COWARD** (1899–1973) was a flamboyant English playwright, actor, composer, and singer. He is known for such plays as *Blythe Spirit* and *Private Lives* and songs like *Mad Dogs and Englishmen* and *Don't Let's be Beastly to the Germans*.

123   **ROBERT CRISP** (1911–94) was a South African–born first class cricketer who joined the British army in the Second World War and served as a tank commander in Greece and the Western Desert, his exploits earning him a Distinguished Service Order and a Military Cross.

37   **VIVANT DENON** (1747–1825) accompanied Napoleon to Egypt; his *Travels in Upper and Lower Egypt*, which he wrote and illustrated, laid the foundations for modern Egyptology. Napoleon later appointed him the first director of the Louvre Museum in Paris.

11   **DIO OF PRUSA** (c.40–c.115), also known as Dio Chrysostom ('golden-mouthed'), was a Greek orator from Prusa, now called Bursa in Turkey. He also wrote a number of philosophical and historical works.

LAWRENCE DURRELL (1912–90) was a British poet and *111, 130* novelist. Born in India and educated in England, he spent most of his life in the lands of the Mediterranean. During the Second World War he was British Information Officer in Alexandria. He is most famous for his novel *The Alexandria Quartet.*

ELIZA FAY (c.1755–1816), born just outside London, *34* traveled to India in 1779. Robbed by Bedouins in Egypt and taken captive on arrival in India, her calamitous journey was interspersed with dedicated bouts of sightseeing observed with a sharp but sentimental eye.

ROBIN FEDDEN (1908–77), who was born in England and *137* raised in France, served as a British diplomat in Athens before the war and a lecturer in English literature in Cairo, where with Lawrence Durrell he founded the literary journal *Personal Landscape.*

96, 97 **E.M. FORSTER** (1879–1970) was the British author of *A Room with a View*, *A Passage to India,* and other novels. During the First World War he worked for the Red Cross in Alexandria, where he met Constantine Cavafy and promoted his poetry. He also wrote *Alexandria: A History and a Guide.*

52 **SARAH HAIGHT** (b. c.1810) was a New York socialite and wife of a well-established merchant who was also president of the American Oriental Society. She was the first American woman to write about Egypt.

21 **IBN BATTUTA** (1304–c.1369), was a Berber from Morocco who in the course of thirty years traveled throughout North and West Africa, Eastern Europe, and the Middle East, Central and Southeast Asia, and beyond. He wrote his *Travels* after his return to Morocco in 1354, where he lived out his life as a judge.

17 **IBN JUBAYR** (1145–1217) was a poet and geographer from Valencia in Arab Spain. In 1183 he made the pilgrimage to Mecca and later wrote about his journeys through Syria, Palestine, and Egypt.

C S Jarvis (1879–1953) was born in London and learned Arabic while serving in the British army in Palestine and Egypt during the First World War. His knowledge of Bedouin ways led to his appointment as governor of Sinai in 1923. He wrote seriously about natural history and humorously about the town life of Egypt.   *101, 103*

R. Talbot Kelly (1861–1934) was an English writer, illustrator, and painter who acquired a studio in Cairo in 1883, became fluent in Arabic, and made the people and landscapes of Egypt the main subject of his life's work.   *77*

François Levernay (b. c.1830) was a French resident of Alexandria who chronicled the rapid economic and industrial development of Egypt in his guide and yearbook published in 1860 and updated in 1872.   *46, 91*

26 **WILLIAM LITHGOW** (1582–c.1645) was a Scotsman of a poor but apparently well educated background with an irresistible desire to visit strange lands. In all he walked 36,000 miles in his lifetime, traveling to Spain and North Africa, across Europe to Greece, and to Palestine and Egypt.

134 **NAGUIB MAHFOUZ** (1911–2006) was an Egyptian writer who won the 1988 Nobel Prize for Literature. His novels, such as *Palace Walk*, *Palace of Desire,* and *Sugar Street*, are usually set in Cairo but *Miramar*, which adopts a new form and is critical of the Nasser regime, is set in Alexandria.

63 **HARRIET MARTINEAU** (1802–76) was an English writer of sociological books, often with a feminist slant. Her visit to Egypt in 1846 led her to find little difference between ancient and modern religious beliefs, which scandalized her usual publisher John Murray, who declined her *Eastern Life*.

46 **JOHN MURRAY** (b. 1745) was the Scottish founder of John Murray publishers in London, which from its inception in 1768 until its takeover by a conglomerate in 2002 was run

by a member of the family whose name was always John Murray. From 1838 the company began publishing its famous *Murray's Handbooks*, with *Egypt* appearing in 1847.

FLORENCE NIGHTINGALE (1820–1910) is famous as the founder of modern nursing. But in 1849, immediately before she first trained as a nurse, she came to Egypt, which she described in a series of vivid letters. In 1854 she went to the Crimea to tend the wounded soldiers there and became world-famous as 'The Lady of the Lamp.'   *68*

FILIPPO PIGAFETTA (1533–1604) was an Italian mathematician and traveler. In his youth he pursued a military career and became an expert in the design and technology of fortifications, an interest that brought him to Egypt.   *24*

PLUTARCH (c.46–120) was a Greek historian and biographer known chiefly for his Lives of ancient Greeks and Romans. He became a Roman citizen and traveled extensively throughout the Mediterranean, visiting both Rome and Alexandria.   *2*

28   **RICHARD POCOCKE** (1704–65) was an Englishman with family connections in the Church of Ireland where he followed a career that left him ample time to travel and satisfy his antiquarian curiosity. His most ambitious journey was to Egypt in 1737–38, which was hardly known to European travelers, where after arriving at Alexandria he went up the Nile as far as Philae.

54   **SOPHIA POOLE** (1804–91) was an English writer, the first to describe from direct observation the private domestic lives of Egyptian women. She was the sister of Edward William Lane, author of *The Modern Egyptians*, and lived with him in Cairo from 1842 to 1849.

47   **HENRY SALT** (1780–1827) was British Consul General in Egypt from 1815 to 1827, where he acquired several collections of antiquities that he sold to the British Museum and the Louvre. Salt helped further knowledge of ancient Egypt through his excavations and his translations of hieroglyphs.

ROBERT SCHINDLER (b. 1899) was the Cairo-based epony-   *112, 117*
mous publisher of *Schindler's Guide to Alexandria* and other
books of travel and local interest in the 1930s and 1940s.

DOUGLAS SLADEN (1856–1947) was born in London,   *86*
became the first professor of history at the University of
Sydney in Australia, and later gave much of his time to traveling and writing. In 1897–99 he was editor of *Who's Who*.

REVEREND A.C. SMITH (b. c.1822) was an English clergy-   *75*
man educated at Eton and Oxford who traveled to Egypt
in the 1860s with his father and another clergyman.

THEODORE STEPHANIDES (1896–1983) was a Greek natu-   *127*
ralist, doctor, poet, and writer. He is best known as the
friend and mentor of the naturalist Gerald Durrell and features in his *My Family and Other Animals*. He also appears
in Lawrence Durrell's *Prospero's Cell* and Henry Miller's
Colossus of Maroussi.

83 **RONALD STORRS** (1881–1955) was a British diplomat, serving as Oriental Secretary in Cairo before the First World War, from 1917 as Governor of Jerusalem, and later as Governor of Cyprus and of Northern Rhodesia. His earliest post, when he lived in Alexandria in 1905, was with the Egyptian Ministry of Finance.

4 **STRABO** (63BC–c.AD24) was a Greek geographer and historian who boasted of having traveled more widely than anyone before him. He has provided the best description of Alexandria that we have from ancient times, but it is frustrating for what he assumes the reader knows and therefore he leaves out.

58 **WILLIAM MAKEPEACE THACKERAY** (1811–63) was born in Calcutta but came to England when he was five. He is famous for his satirical novels such as *Vanity Fair,* which he began immediately after a three-month Mediterranean cruise described in *From Cornhill to Grand Cairo.*

MARK TWAIN (1835–1910) was an American writer, the   *73*
author of *The Adventures of Tom Sawyer* and *The Adventures
of Huckleberry Finn*. These were preceded by *The Innocents
Abroad*, his account of a five-month cruise of Europe and the
Middle East, one of the best-selling travel books of all time.

GWYN WILLIAMS (1904–90), a Welshman, taught for many   *113*
years at Cairo University until, in 1943, he was made professor of English literature at Alexandria University. He was
a close friend of Lawrence Durrell's throughout the war.

GASTON ZANANIRI (1904–96) was an Alexandrian writer of   *139*
Jewish and Syrian Christian descent: he became a Domini-
can friar in Paris in his later years. He was a close friend of
Constantine Cavafy's in the 1920s and a friend of Lawrence Durrell in the 1940s.

COUNT PATRICE DE ZOGHEB (b. c.1885) was of a Lebanese   *85*
Christian family long settled in Alexandria. Their property
holdings were extensive; in one of their large town houses,
the Okel Zogheb, the poet Constantine Cavafy was born.

Bibliography

Abd al-Latif al-Baghdadi, *Relation de l'Egypte par Abd al-Latif*, trans. Silvestre de Sacy, Paris, 1810.

Abd al-Malik ibn Juraij, quoted in Alfred J. Butler, *The Arab Conquest of Egypt*, Oxford: Oxford University Press, 1902.

Amr ibn al-As, quoted in Alfred J. Butler, *The Arab Conquest of Egypt*, Oxford: Oxford University Press, 1902.

Baedeker, Karl, *Egypt: Handbook for Travellers*, 2nd edition, Leipzig, 1885

Baedeker, Karl, *Egypt: Handbook for Travellers*, 5th edition, Leipzig, 1902.

Breccia, Evaristo, *Alexandrea ad Aegyptum*, Bergamo, 1922.

Brinton, Jasper, unpublished diaries, Alexandria, 1926, quoted in Michael Haag, *Alexandria: City of Memory*, Cairo: The American University in Cairo Press, 2004.

Brinton, Josie, ["At the Movies"] letter to her mother, 8 March 1937, quoted in Michael Haag, *Alexandria: City of Memory*, Cairo: The American University in Cairo Press, 2004.

Brinton, Josie, ["An Air Raid Alert"] unpublished diaries, 1941, quoted in Michael Haag, *Alexandria: City of Memory*, Cairo: The American University in Cairo Press, 2004.

Brocardo, Pegregrino, in G. Lumbroso, *Descrittori italiani dell'Egitto e di Alessandria*, 1879, trans. Giovanni Curatola and quoted in

Anthony Hirst and M.S. Silk, *Alexandria Real and Imagined*, Farnham: Ashgate 2004.

Bruce, James, *Travels to Discover the Source of the Nile in the Years 1768, 1769, 1770, 1771, 1772, and 1773*. Edinburgh and London: G.G.J. and J. Robinson, 1790.

Butcher, Edith Louisa, *Things Seen in Egypt*, London, 1914.

Caillard, Mabel, *A Lifetime in Egypt*, London: Grant Richards, 1935.

Carne, John, *Letters from the East*, London 1826.

Cavafy, C.P., ["The Graeco-Roman Museum"] *Selected Prose Works*, trans. Peter Jeffreys, Ann Arbor: The University of Michigan Press, 2010.

Cavafy, C.P. ["View from His Balcony"], quoted in Michael Haag, *Alexandria: City of Memory*, Cairo: The American University in Cairo Press, 2004.

Cavafy, C.P. ["The God Abandons Antony"], trans. George Valassopoulos, in E.M. Forster, *Alexandria: A History and a Guide*, Alexandria, 1922.

Cocteau, Jean, *Maalesh*, trans. Mary C. Hoeck, London: Peter Owen, 1956.

de Cosson, Anthony, *Mareotis*, London: Country Life Ltd., 1935.

Coward, Noël, *Middle East Diary*, London: William Heinemann Ltd, 1944.

Crisp, Robert, *The Gods Were Neutral*, London: Frederick Muller Ltd, 1960.

Denon, Vivant, *Travels in Upper and Lower Egypt*, trans. Arthur Aikin, London: Longman and Rees, 1803.

Dio of Prusa (Dio Chrysostom), Loeb Classical Library, Cambridge: Harvard University Press, 1940.

Durrell, Lawrence ["The Dream-City Alexandria"], introduction to E.M. Forster, *Alexandria: A History and a Guide*, London: Michael Haag Ltd., 1980.

Durrell, Lawrence ["War Effort"], letter to Henry Miller, May 1944, *Durrell–Miller Letters*, London: Faber and Faber / Michael Haag, 1988.

Fay, Eliza, *Original Letters from India (1779–1815): Mrs Eliza Fay*, ed. E.M. Forster, London: Hogarth Press, 1925.

Fedden, Robin, *Egypt: Land of the Valley*, London: John Murray, 1977.

Forster, E.M. *The Egyptian Mail*, 1917.

Haight, Sarah, *Letters from the Old World*, New York, 1840.

Ibn Battuta, *Travels in Asia and Africa 1325–1354*, tr. and ed. H.A.R. Gibb, London: Broadway House, 1929.

Ibn Jubayr, *Travels*, trans. R.J.C. Broadhurst. London: Jonathan Cape, 1952.

Jarvis, C.S., *Oriental Spotlight*, London: John Murray, 1937.

Kelly, R. Talbot, *Egypt: Painted and Described*, London: Adam and Charles Black, 1912.

Levernay, François, *Guide et Annuaire d'Egypte*, 1872, trans. Colin Clement in *Alexandria 1860–1960*, Alexandria: Harpocrates Press, 1997.

Lithgow, William, *Rare Adventures and Painful Peregrinations*, London 1632.

Mahfouz, Naguib, *Miramar*, trans. Fatma Moussa Mahmoud, Cairo: The American University in Cairo Press, 1978.

Martineau, Harriet, *Eastern Life, Present and Past*, London: Edward Moxon, 1848.

Murray's *Handbook to Egypt*, London: John Murray, 1847

Nightingale, Florence, *Letters from Egypt*, London: Barrie and Jenkins, 1987.

Pigafetta, Filippo, *Viaggio o itinerario dell'Egitto e delle Arabia*, trans. Giovanni Curatola and quoted in Anthony Hirst and M.S.Silk, *Alexandria Real and Imagined*, Farnham: Ashgate 2004.

Plutarch, *Alexander* (*Lives*, Vol. VII), Loeb Classical Library, trans. Bernadotte Perrin, Cambridge: Harvard University Press, 1919.

Pocock, Richard, *A Description of the East and Some Other Countries*, Volume 1: *Observations on Egypt*, London 1743.

Poole, Sophia, *The Englishwoman in Egypt*, London: Charles Knight & Co., 1844.

Salt, Henry, letter to William Hamilton, Alexandria, 27 March 1816, in J.J. Halls, *The Life and Correspondence of Henry Salt*, London 1834.

Schindler's *Guide to Alexandria*, Cairo: Schindler, 1943.

Sladen, Douglas, *Queer Things About Egypt*, London 1910.

Smith, Reverend A.C., *The Nile and Its Banks: A Journal of Travels in Egypt and Nubia*, London 1868.

Stephanides, Theodore, *Autumn Gleanings*, Corfu: Durrell School of Corfu / Pine Bluff: International Lawrence Durrell Society, 2011.

Storrs, Ronald, *Orientations*, London, 1937.

Strabo, *Book XVII*, Loeb Classical Library, Cambridge: Harvard University Press, 1932.

Thackeray, W.M., *Cornhill to Cairo*, London, 1845.

Twain, Mark, *Innocents Abroad,* Hartford, 1869.

Williams, Gwyn, *ABC of (D.)G.W.*, Llandysul: Gomer Press, 1981.

Zananiri, Gaston, quoted in Michael Haag, *Alexandria: City of Memory*, Cairo: The American University in Cairo Press, 2004.

de Zogheb, Patrice, *Alexandria Memories*, Alexandria, 1949.

Acknowledgments

The editor and publisher acknowledge with thanks the permission to use material in this book from the following: Alice Brinton for excepts from the diaries and letters of Judge Jasper Brinton and Josie Brinton. Giovanni Curatola for his translation of excerpts from the works of Peregrino Brocardo and Filippo Pigafetta in *Alexandria Real and Imagined*. Peter Jeffreys for his translation of an excerpt from Constantine Cavafy's "Our Museum" in C.P. Cavafy, *Selected Prose Works*. Laura Lightbody for the translation by George Valassopoulos of Constantine Cavafy's "The God Abandons Antony." Peter Owen Ltd for an excerpt from Jean Cocteau's *Maalesh*. Alan Brodie Representation Ltd, www.alanbrodie.com, for excerpts from Nöel Coward's *Middle East Diary* © NC Aventales AG 1944. Jonathan Crisp for excerpts from Robert Crisp's *The Gods Were Neutral*. The Estate of Lawrence Durrell and Curtis Brown Ltd for excerpts from Lawrence Durrell's letters and his introduction to E.M. Forster's *Alexandria: A History and a Guide*. Frances Fedden for an excerpt from Robin Fedden's *Egypt: Land of the Valley*. The Random House Group for excerpts from R.J.C. Broadhurst's translation of *The Travels of Ibn Jubayr*. Colin Clement for his translation of François Levernay's *Guide et Annuaire d'Egypte*, 1872, in *Alexandria 1860–1960*. The American University in Cairo Press for excerpts from Naguib Mahfouz's *Miramar*. Alexia Stephanides Mercouri for excerpts from Theodore Stephanides' *Autumn Gleanings*. Gwyd Williams for excerpts from Gwyn Williams' *The ABC of (D)GW*. The Alexandria and Mediterranean Research Center at the Bibliotheca Alexandrina for an excerpt from Count Patrice de Zogheb's *Alexandria Memories*.

Illustration Sources

The illustrations in this volume are taken from Michael Haag, *Vintage Alexandria: Photographs of the City, 1860–1960* (AUC Press, 2008), with the exception of: front cover, 33, 60: *Description de l'Egypte*, 1809–1818 (courtesy of the Rare Books and Special Collections Library of the American University in Cairo); 1: Hermann Thiersch, *Pharos, Antike, Islam und Occident*, 1909; 16: Richard Pococke, *A Description of the East and Some Other Countries, Volume 1: Observations on Egypt*, 1743; 23, 37: Vivant Denon, *Travels in Upper and Lower Egypt*, 1803 (courtesy of the Rare Books and Special Collections Library of the American University in Cairo); 27: G. Braun and F. Hogenberg, *Civitates Orbis Terrarum*, 1572–90; 53 and back cover: F.L. Norden, *Voyage d'Egypte et de Nubie*, 1755; 78: Michael Haag collection.